By the **NuMbErs**

>>> The world record for **fastest speed** on a **snowboard** is just over **125 miles an hour!**

(201 km/h)

NATIONAL
GEOGRAPHIC
KiDS

WASHINGTON, D.C.

What is an **INFOGRAPHIC?**
And what's this book **ALL ABOUT?**

A number is just a number, right? Nope! This book is all about bringing numbers to life so you can understand the story behind the figures. So you won't see boring old numbers written out on the page, you'll see them in cool photos, awesome illustrations, wacky graphs, and fascinating charts. How, you might ask? One word: Infographics.

Also called information graphics, these are visual illustrations of information and data. These graphics show sometimes confusing numbers in a quick, fun, and uncomplicated way. Infographics come in a bunch of different shapes, sizes, patterns, and colors, and you'll find them all in this book. So get ready to be amazed, surprised, and completely captivated. You're about to see numbers, data, and statistics like you've never seen them before.

Infographics in this book:

PHOTO INFOGRAPHICS
Beautiful photos are used in this infographic to illustrate numbers and data, while pop-outs present the facts behind the figures. See pages 50-51 and 106-107.

WORD CLOUDS
It is exactly like how it sounds—a cloud of words, where each word's size varies. Word clouds represent the concept of frequency in math and statistics—the bigger the number, the more important it is. See pages 12-13.

HEAT MAPS
Instead of listing numbers, a heat or chloropleth map substitutes colors for digits. The darker the color, the higher the number, concentration, percentage, or whatever is being shown on the page. See pages 46-47.

PIE CHARTS

Surely you've seen a pie before. Imagine it split up into slices, with each section representing a specific percentage of the whole. Voilà! You've got yourself a pie chart. See pages 18-19 and 130-131.

VISUAL ARTICLES

Have you ever read something that seems too confusing to grasp? That's where visual articles are most useful. These are infographics that turn long articles with lots of information into visual data that you can understand and digest quickly. See pages 70-71 and 92-93.

VERSUS OR COMPARISON INFOGRAPHICS

Here, a battle takes place between two or more things, drawn out so we can visually see their similarities and differences. See pages 40-41 and 226-227.

GRAPHS

These are classic bar graphs showing the relationship between quantities that you might use in school, laid out on x and y axes, but we've spiced them up a bit for you. See pages 56-57 and 124-125.

BUBBLE CHARTS

These infographics display data in the form of bubbles or other objects, where the biggest ones represent the biggest numbers. A comparison of size clearly conveys the differences among the data points. See pages 78-79 and 146-147.

TIME LINES

These are stories illustrated through chronological dates that will take you on a journey from start to finish. See pages 62-63.

Meet the EXPERTS!

ALSO FEATURED IN *BY THE NUMBERS* IS EVERYTHING YOU WANTED TO KNOW ABOUT COOL PEOPLE WORKING IN THE FIELD OF MATH AND NUMBERS. CHECK THEM OUT TO GET ADVICE ON MATH, SCIENCE, AND HOW TO BECOME A NUMBERS WHIZ. PLUS, LEARN EXACTLY WHAT MAKES THEIR JOBS SO AWESOME.

EXTREME ROLLER COASTERS

Got a stomach of steel?

You'll need one if you climb aboard one of these three roller coasters that boost the fear factor.

GOLIATH

GURNEE, ILLINOIS, U.S.A.

HEIGHT:

165 FEET (50 M)

SPEED:

72 MPH (116 KM/H)

INSANE FACTOR:

The world's tallest, fastest, and steepest wooden roller coaster has a 180-foot (55-m) vertical drop that ends in an underground tunnel.

BANSHEE
MASON, OHIO, U.S.A.

TWISTED COLOSSUS
VALENCIA, CALIFORNIA, U.S.A.

HEIGHT:
121 FEET (37 M)

SPEED:
57 MPH (92 KM/H)

HEIGHT:
170 FEET (52 M)

SPEED:
68 MPH (109 KM/H)

INSANE FACTOR:
The world's longest inverted steel roller coaster is **4,124 feet (1,257 m)** long and has **7** inversions.

INSANE FACTOR:
This ride's two trains pass each other at different points, giving the **illusion that riders could high-five** when they pass each other.

HEART

46 POUNDS (21 KG)

HEIGHT

13 FEET (4 M)

SKIN

1.5 INCHES (3.8 CM) THICK

FOOD

300 POUNDS (136 KG) PER DAY

8

Nothing is small about an adult male African elephant. From head to toe, the max stats on **Earth's biggest land animal are huge!**

BRAIN

12 POUNDS (5.4 KG)

EARS

100 POUNDS (45 KG) EACH

LIFE SPAN UP TO

70 YEARS

TUSKS

100 POUNDS (45 KG) EACH

TRUNK MUSCLES

100,000

TOTAL WEIGHT

14,000 POUNDS (6,350 KG)

LETTUCE
1 week

10

CHICKEN
2 to 3 days

EGGS
4 to 5 weeks

STEAK
3 to 5 days

Knowing how long it takes food to spoil means you could lower your chances of wasting food again. Check out what goes bad quickly and what can last longer in your fridge.

PEAR
5 days

FRESH SHRIMP
1 to 2 days

MILK
8 to 20 days

BREAD
1 to 2 weeks

FRESH BROCCOLI
3 to 5 days

MAYONNAISE
2 months

FAVORITE FLAVORS

COOKIES AND CREAM 3.6%

CHOCOLATE MARSHMALLOW 1.3%

butter pecan 5.3%

NEAPOLITAN 4.2%

CHOCOLATE
ALMOND 1.6%

CHOCOLATE CHIP 3.9%

ROCKY
ROAD 1.5%

PRALINE
PECAN 1.7%

VANILLA FUDGE
RIPPLE 2.6%

strawberry 5.3%

CHOCOLATE 8.9%

VANILLA 29%

CHERRY 1.6%

FRENCH
VANILLA 3.8%

SNOW flavored with honey and fruit was an EARLY VERSION OF ICE CREAM eaten by the ancient Greeks.

The average person in the UNITED STATES EATS MORE ICE CREAM a year—38.7 PINTS (18 L)—than anywhere else in the world. The average Australian consumes 20.5 PINTS (9.7 L) of ice cream a year.

What's your favorite ice-cream flavor?

This tasty word cloud shows the percentage of people who chose each flavor as their favorite. The bigger the word, the more popular the flavor.

Yum!

ONE
SUMATRAN TIGER

WEIGHS AS MUCH AS

66

HOUSE CATS

RACE TO THE FINISH

Some animals use camouflage
to hide from predators, others use stealth. And some use speed! But who's the fastest, human or animal?

GREYHOUND

43 MPH
(69 km/h)

USAIN BOLT, RUNNER

27 MPH
(44 km/h)

NORTH AFRICAN OSTRICH

40 MPH
(64 km/h)

PRONGHORN

55 MPH

(89 km/h)

Usain Bolt ran **328 feet** (100 m) in **9.58 seconds** in Germany in 2009. A cheetah in a Cincinnati, Ohio, U.S.A., zoo was clocked at **5.95 seconds** running the same distance.

CHEETAH

61 MPH

(98 km/h)

THOROUGHBRED RACEHORSE

55 MPH (89 km/h)

PET OWNERSHIP IN THE U.S.A.

Ever wondered how many pet dogs or cats are out there? Check out this chart, which shows counts of some of the most popular pets in the United States. This may seem like a lot of households, but remember, some families own both a dog and a cat ... or more than one of each!

NUMBER OF HOUSEHOLDS WITH CATS:
36,117,000

NUMBER OF HOUSEHOLDS WITH HORSES:
1,780,000

NUMBER OF HOUSEHOLDS WITH BIRDS:
3,671,000

NUMBER OF HOUSEHOLDS
WITH FISH:
7,738,000

NUMBER OF HOUSEHOLDS
WITH HAMSTERS:
877,000

NUMBER OF HOUSEHOLDS
WITH DOGS:
43,346,000

SEASONS IN SPACE

Scorching summers, wild winters—each of Earth's four seasons is about 90 days long. But imagine if summer were to last years, not months. Most of the other planets in our solar system have longer seasons than ours because of their rotation, orbit, distance from the sun, and axial tilt. See how long one season on other planets lasts.

MARS
7 MONTHS

EARTH
90 DAYS

MERCURY
0
THERE ARE NO SEASONAL DIFFERENCES ON MERCURY

VENUS
55-58 DAYS

JUPITER
3
YEARS

URANUS
21
YEARS

SATURN
8
YEARS

NEPTUNE
41
YEARS

0.008–0.01 INCH
(0.2–0.3 mm)

SIZING UP BUGS

Insects and other bugs are everywhere, from flakes of your skin to the slopes of Mount Everest. But they also come in many different sizes. Check out some of the largest and smallest insects!

RHINOCEROS BEETLE

7.9 INCHES
(20 cm)

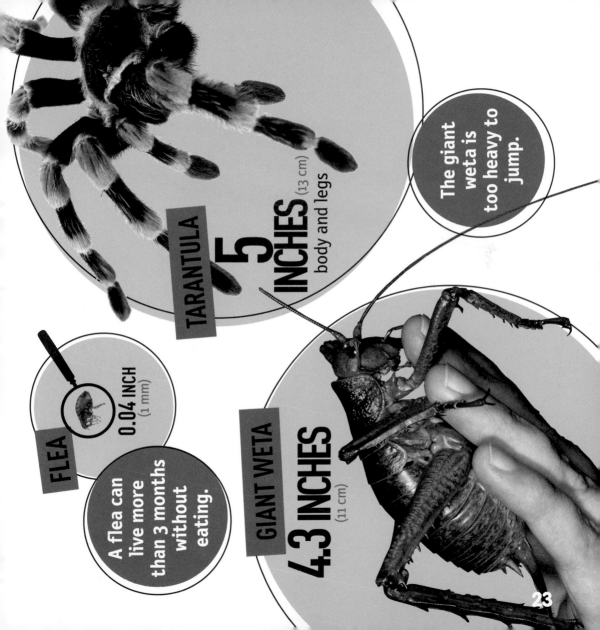

TARANTULA

5 INCHES (13 cm)
body and legs

The giant weta is too heavy to jump.

FLEA

0.04 INCH (1 mm)

A flea can live more than 3 months without eating.

GIANT WETA

4.3 INCHES (11 cm)

23

THE PEEP FORMULA

IT TAKES **6 MINUTES** TO MAKE A MARSHMALLOW CHICK FROM START TO FINISH. (WHEN THEY WERE FIRST MADE IN **1953,** IT TOOK **27 HOURS.**)

FACTORY MACHINES CAN APPLY **3,500** PEEP EYES IN **1 MINUTE.**

ABOUT **2 BILLION** PEEPS ARE MADE EVERY YEAR— ENOUGH TO CIRCLE EARTH **2 TIMES.**

TO PRODUCE PEEPS QUICKLY, SPECIAL MACHINERY MAKES SHEETS OF **6 ROWS** OF PEEPS WITH **5 PER ROW.**

 PEEPS STAY FRESH ON THE SHELF FOR **2 YEARS.**

DURING THE FIRST **2 YEARS** OF PRODUCTION, **PEEPS HAD WINGS.**

IN **1955** THEIR WINGS WERE TAKEN OFF FOR A **SLEEKER LOOK.**

ON NEW YEAR'S EVE, THE TOWN OF BETHLEHEM, PENNSYLVANIA, U.S.A., DROPS A **100-POUND** (45-KG) PEEP TO RING IN THE NEW YEAR.

BODY BASICS

Your body is an amazing machine that gives you the speed you need on the field, and the smarts to ace that exam. But just how cool is it? Here's a look at some of your body's awesome numbers.

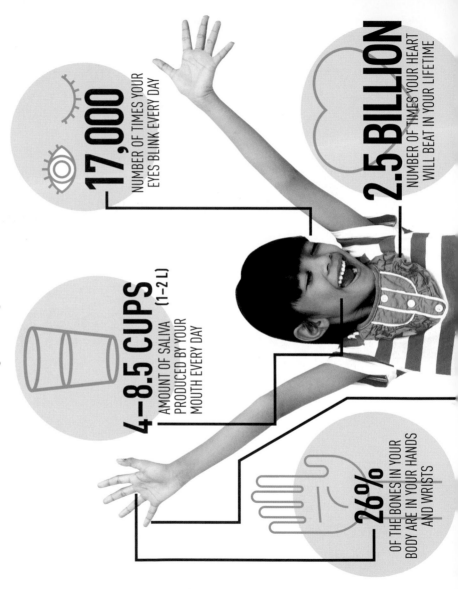

17,000
NUMBER OF TIMES YOUR EYES BLINK EVERY DAY

2.5 BILLION
NUMBER OF TIMES YOUR HEART WILL BEAT IN YOUR LIFETIME

4–8.5 CUPS (1–2 L)
AMOUNT OF SALIVA PRODUCED BY YOUR MOUTH EVERY DAY

26%
OF THE BONES IN YOUR BODY ARE IN YOUR HANDS AND WRISTS

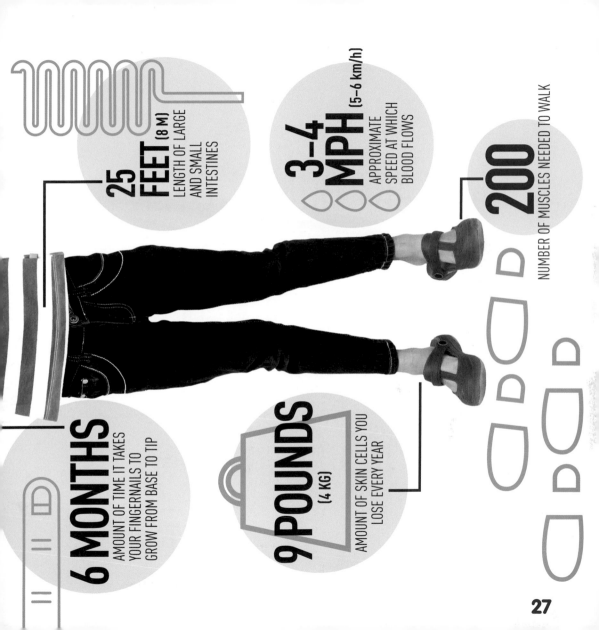

25 FEET (8 M) LENGTH OF LARGE AND SMALL INTESTINES

3–4 MPH (5–6 km/h) APPROXIMATE SPEED AT WHICH BLOOD FLOWS

200 NUMBER OF MUSCLES NEEDED TO WALK

6 MONTHS AMOUNT OF TIME IT TAKES YOUR FINGERNAILS TO GROW FROM BASE TO TIP

9 POUNDS (4 KG) AMOUNT OF SKIN CELLS YOU LOSE EVERY YEAR

27

YOUR HEART PUMPS OVER

1,500 G

OF BLOOD EACH DAY—

ALLONS

(5,678 L)

ENOUGH TO FILL
40 BATHTUBS.

Major League Baseball teams pay their players, of course, but not all teams pay the same amount. Check out this graphic of the top teams with the highest payrolls in 2014. The larger the baseball, the more money the team pays out. **Play ball!**

BOSTON RED SOX
$162,817,411

PHILADELPHIA PHILLIES
$180,052,723

NY YANKEES
$203,812,506

L.A. DODGERS
$235,295,219

Babe Ruth hit 54 home runs during the 1920 season. Only one team hit more home runs that year than Babe did by himself.

Each regulation baseball has 108 red double stitches (or 216 single stitches).

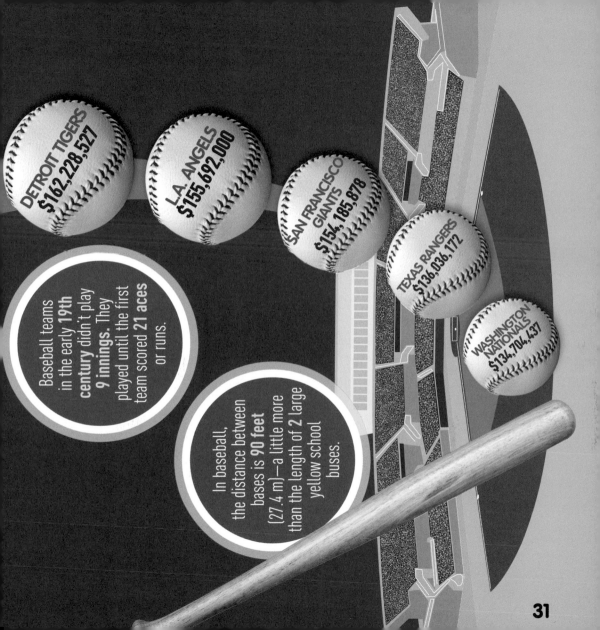

DETROIT TIGERS
$162,228,527

L.A. ANGELS
$155,692,000

SAN FRANCISCO GIANTS
$154,185,878

TEXAS RANGERS
$136,036,172

WASHINGTON NATIONALS
$134,704,437

Baseball teams in the early **19th century** didn't play **9 innings.** They played until the first team scored **21 aces** or runs.

In baseball, the distance between bases is **90 feet** (27.4 m)—a little more than the length of 2 large yellow school buses.

FLASH STATS ABOUT LIGHTNING

Ever wondered about those amazing flashing bolts in the sky?
Hot, powerful, and fast—the statistics surrounding lightning are truly electric.

If you count the seconds in between a flash of lightning and the crack of thunder then divide by **5** you get the number of miles lightning is away from you.

The average lightning bolt is about **1 inch wide.** (2.5 cm)

The return stroke of a lightning bolt—which goes from the ground back up to the clouds—travels at **220,000,000 miles an hour.** (554,000,000 km/h)

The longest lightning bolt—recorded in Texas—was **118 miles long.** (190 km)

There are about **8 million** lightning strikes on Earth every day.

The air temperature around lightning can reach

50,000 (27,700°C)

degrees Fahrenheit. That's **5 times** hotter than the surface of the sun.

A lightning bolt is an explosive discharge of electricity that is on average

5 miles

long. (8 km)

The average lightning bolt could power a

100-watt

bulb for **3 months.**

A former U.S. National Park Service ranger survived being struck by lightning

7 times.

The odds that a person living in the U.S. will be struck by lightning are

1 in 12,000.

It is Chinese tradition to wait to name a panda cub until it's **100** days old.

GIGANTIC NUMBERS ABOUT PANDAS

Pandas need our protection. Only about 1,800 live in the wild, and more than 300 live in zoos and breeding centers, mostly in China. Yet there's so much to love about these roly-poly mammals. So take a look at some big numbers about these beloved and endangered black-and-white bears.

BORN HAIRLESS AND BLIND, NEWBORN PANDAS ARE 1/900 THE SIZE OF THEIR MOM.

A WILD GIANT PANDA'S DIET IS 99% BAMBOO.

CUBS DON'T OPEN THEIR EYES UNTIL THEY ARE BETWEEN 6 AND 8 WEEKS OLD.

MALES WEIGH UP TO 250 POUNDS (113 KG). FEMALES NO MORE THAN 220 POUNDS (100 KG).

PANDAS HAVE TO SPEND UP TO 16 HOURS A DAY FORAGING AND EATING.

TO GET ALL THE NUTRIENTS THEY NEED, PANDAS EAT AS MUCH AS

44 POUNDS (20 KG) OF BAMBOO A DAY.

CUBS STAY WITH THEIR MOTHERS FOR UP TO 3 YEARS BEFORE HEADING OUT ON THEIR OWN.

GIANT PANDAS LIVE IN HIGH-ELEVATION FORESTS AT 5,000–10,000 FEET (1,524–3,048 M)

WHEN STANDING ON ALL FOUR LEGS, PANDAS ARE 2–3 FEET (0.6–0.9 M) TALL AT THE SHOULDER—ABOUT THE SIZE OF AN AMERICAN BLACK BEAR.

"WE INVENTED MATH AND ART FOR THE SAME REASON: TO HELP US UNDERSTAND THE WORLD AROUND US, AND WHAT IT'S LIKE TO BE A HUMAN BEING. THERE ARE ALL KINDS OF WAYS YOU CAN USE MATH TO MAKE ART, AND ALL KINDS OF WAYS YOU CAN USE ART TO THINK ABOUT MATH. THEY GO TOGETHER REALLY WELL!"

AN INTERVIEW WITH JER THORP

Q: WHAT IS IT THAT YOU DO?
A: I'm a data artist—I make art from numbers!

Q: WHAT'S THE COOLEST PIECE OF ART YOU'VE EVER MADE?
A: Two years ago, I collaborated with my mom to make a 30-foot (9-m)-long woven tapestry called Infinite Weft. It was made with a special mathematical formula that makes it so the pattern in the fabric will never repeat—not even if it stretched all the way to the moon!

Q: WHAT IS IT ABOUT NUMBERS THAT FASCINATES YOU?
A: Everything you see and touch is full of hidden patterns. As humans we have learned to describe these patterns through numbers. In doing this, we understand much more about our world. Numbers are like magic keys to the world's most exciting things.

The background of this page is a piece from Thorp's Infinite Weft tapestry.

IN-DEPTH OCEAN NUMBERS

The world's oceans cover 70 percent of Earth's surface—but what lies beneath those waters? It depends on how low you go!

830' (253 M)
Free dive record (one breath of air, no oxygen tanks)

1,044' (318 M)
Scuba dive record

3,280' (1,000 M)
Deepest that sunlight can travel in the ocean and where colossal squid swim

7,920' (2,414 M)
Where giant tube worms live

830'
1,044'
3,280'
7,920'
12,476'

12,467'
[3,800 M]

Titanic wreckage

27,454'
[8,368 M]

Where cusk eel live, deepest swimming fish

The pressure at the deepest part of the ocean is **8 tons** (11,270,000 kg/sq m) per square inch. That's the equivalent of trying to hold **50 jumbo jets!**

36,000'
[10,970 M]

Mariana Trench, the deepest part of the ocean

27,454'

36,000'

One is the king of the jungle, the other the largest of the 4 big cats. Both are formidable hunters. But how do they stack up?

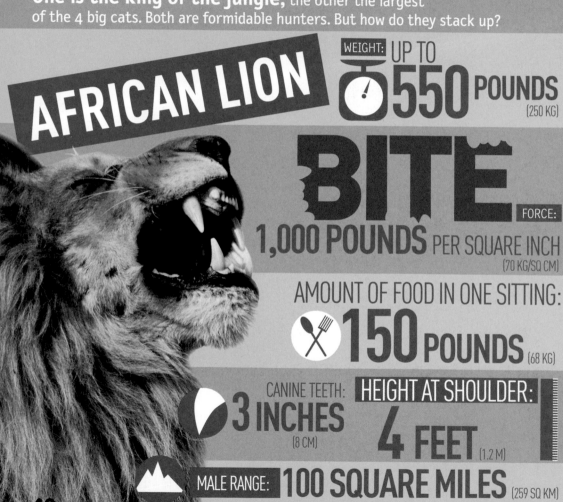

AFRICAN LION

WEIGHT: UP TO **550** POUNDS (250 KG)

BITE FORCE: **1,000 POUNDS** PER SQUARE INCH (70 KG/SQ CM)

AMOUNT OF FOOD IN ONE SITTING: **150** POUNDS (68 KG)

CANINE TEETH: **3 INCHES** (8 CM)

HEIGHT AT SHOULDER: **4 FEET** (1.2 M)

MALE RANGE: **100 SQUARE MILES** (259 SQ KM)

SIBERIAN TIGER

WEIGHT: UP TO

845 POUNDS
(383 KG)

BITE
FORCE:
1,000 POUNDS PER SQUARE INCH
(70 KG/SQ CM)

AMOUNT OF FOOD IN ONE SITTING:

60 POUNDS (27 KG)

CANINE TEETH:
4 INCHES
(10 CM)

HEIGHT AT SHOULDER:
3 FEET (0.9 M)

IT'S A **TIE!**

 MALE RANGE: **400 SQUARE MILES** (1,036 SQ KM)

ah," said Harry.

ut he didn't get the job, did he?" said Hermione. "So he never
he chance to find a founder's object there and hide it in the

ol!"

kay, then," said ... feated. "Forget Hogwarts."

Vithout any o... ...aveled into London and, hidden
eath the Invis... ...hed for the orphanage in which
demort had be... ...one stole into a library and dis-
ered from their re... ...he place had been demolished many
rs before. They visited its site and found a tower block of offices.

"We could try digging in the foundations?" Hermi...

lfheartedly.

"He wouldn't have hidden a Horcrux here," ...
nown it all along: The orphanage had been ...
d been determined to escape; he would neve...
f his soul there. Dumbledore had shown Har...
ught grandeur or mystique in his hiding places; ...
orner of Londo... ...far removed as you could imagine ...
Hogwarts or... ...building like Gringotts, the Wizard-
ng bank, w... ...and marble floors.

Even wit... ...they continued to move through
the countrysi... ...tent in a different place each night for
security. Every morning they made sure that they had removed all
clues to their presence, then set off to find another lonely and se-
cluded spot, traveling by Apparition to more woods, to the shadowy
crevices of cliffs, to purple moors, gorse-covered mountainsides,
and once a sheltered and pebbly cove. Every twelve hours or so they
passed the Horcrux between them as though they were playing some
perverse, slow-motion game of pass-the-parcel, where they dreaded

Hogwarts was founded ca A.D. 1000

Harry Potter and the Deathly Hallows is the longest book at 784 pages and 197,651 words.

Dumbledore lived to be 115 years old.

---

the music stopping be... ...welve hours of i...
fear and anxiety....

Harry's scar kept... ...ost often, he
when he was wearing... ...mes he could
himself reacting to the p...

"What? What did you see?" demanded Ron, whenever h

Harry wince.

"A face," muttered Harry, every time. "The same face.
who stole from Gregorovitch."

And Ron would turn away, making no effort to hide ...
pointment. Harry knew that Ron was hoping to hear n...
family or of the rest of the Order of the Phoenix, but a...
Harry, was not a television aerial; he could only see what ...
was thinking at the time, not ... ...r took his ...
parently Voldemort was ... ...unkn...
with the gleeful face, wh... ...Har...
Voldemort knew no b... ...sca...
to burn and the merry, ...talia...
memory, he learned to su... ...or dis...
the other two showed nothing ... ...at the m...
thief. He could not entirely blame them, when they we...
ate for a lead on the Horcruxes.

As the days stretched in... ...egan to ...
Ron and Hermione were ... ...ithou...
him. Several times they ... ...wh...
tired the tent, and twice ... ...on th...
a little distance away, hea... ...g fas...
they fell silent when they re... ...pproach ...
hastened to appear busy collecting wood or water.

For the movie, Harry's scar was painted on about 5,800 times.

On the first day the Order of the Phoenix book was available for purchase in 2003, 1,679,753 were sold.

Hermione got 112% on her charms exams during her 1st year at Hogwarts.

HARRY POTTER NUMBERS THAT CAST A SPELL

The 7 Harry Potter books have been read and re-read, and the 8 movies have mesmerized fans around the world. But while the franchise has soared higher than the towers of Hogwarts—with an amusement park, clothes, an online virtual world, and more—the figures behind the books that started it all might just have a little magic in them.

Harry Potter and J. K. Rowling share the same birthday: July 31.

More than 400 million books have been sold in the entire series.

Lord Voldemort was 71 years old when he and Harry dueled at the "Battle of Hogwarts" in *Deathly Hallows*.

J. K. Rowling is the first author to make $1,000,000,000 for writing books.

There are 7 books in the Harry Potter series; students spend 7 years at Hogwarts; Harry Potter's Quidditch number is 7.

Ron Weasley was the 6th out of 7 Weasley kids.

TOP 10 MOST COMMON COMPLETE SENTENCES FROM ALL 7 BOOKS

1 Nothing happened.
2 Harry looked around.
3 Harry stared.
4 He waited.
5 Harry said nothing.
6 They looked at each other.
7 Harry blinked.
8 He looked around.
9 Something he didn't have last time.
10 He stood up.

SUMMING UP **SKATEBOARDS**

1 PIECE OF WOOD IS MADE INTO THIN LAYERS, CALLED **VENEERS**.

7 LAYERS OF VENEER ARE COATED WITH GLUE.

LAYERS **1**, **2**, **4**, **6**, AND **7** HAVE THE GRAIN OF THE WOOD RUNNING FROM THE FRONT OF THE BOARD TO THE BACK; THE **3rd** AND **5th** LAYERS HAVE THE GRAIN RUNNING SIDE TO SIDE.

THE LAYERS OF **VENEER** ARE STACKED AND PUT INTO A PRESS, AND **5** TO **15** BOARDS CAN BE MADE AT ONE TIME. THE STACKS ARE LEFT IN THE PRESS FOR A **FEW MINUTES** TO A **FEW HOURS**.

8 HOLES ARE DRILLED IN THE BOARD TO MOUNT THE TRUCKS. THE DECK IS HAND-SANDED, COATED WITH PAINT, AND **DESIGNS ARE ADDED.**

ALUMINUM BLOCKS ARE HEATED TO **1300°F** [706.7°C] **IN A FURNACE** AND THEN POURED INTO A MOLD TO MAKE THE TRUCK. THE TRUCK IS **HAND-ASSEMBLED** TO THE DECK.

4 WHEELS ARE MADE.

8 **THE SKATEBOARD** IS ASSEMBLED!

1

2

3

4

5

6

7

Have you ever heard, "Eat your fruit and veggies," at your dinner table? While you might feel sneaky heading for dessert instead of your broccoli, adults in each U.S. state reach for healthy fruits and vegetables at different rates. See how your state munches in this tasty graphic.

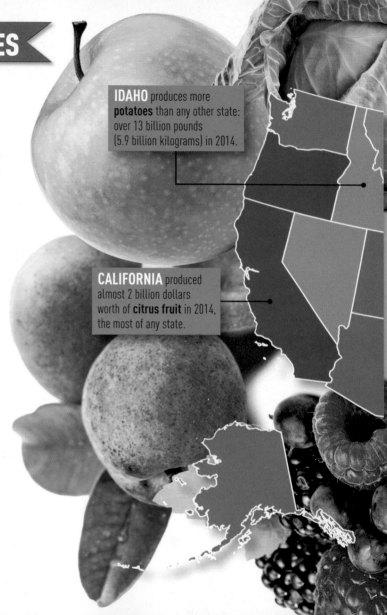

IDAHO produces more **potatoes** than any other state: over 13 billion pounds (5.9 billion kilograms) in 2014.

CALIFORNIA produced almost 2 billion dollars worth of **citrus fruit** in 2014, the most of any state.

KEY

Times per day adults eat fruits and vegetables

- 1.8 or more
- 1.7
- 1.6
- 1.5
- fewer than 1.5

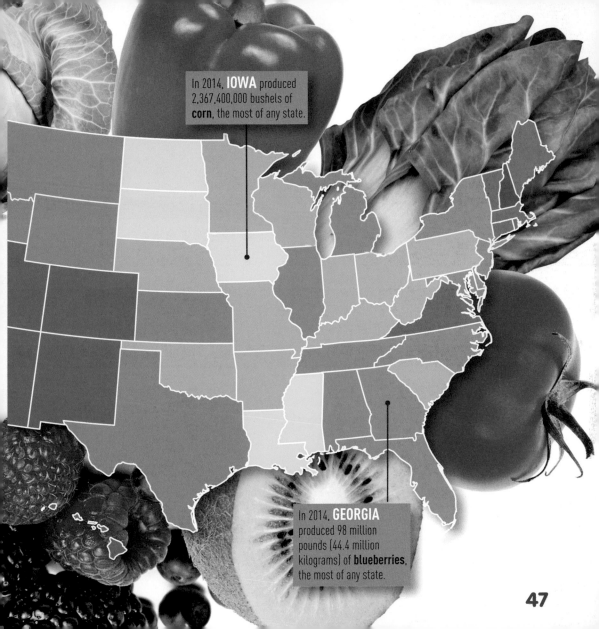

In 2014, **IOWA** produced 2,367,400,000 bushels of **corn**, the most of any state.

In 2014, **GEORGIA** produced 98 million pounds (44.4 million kilograms) of **blueberries**, the most of any state.

47

A MELTING WORLD

If all the ice on Earth melted, the world's oceans would rise 216 feet (66 m). But how high is that exactly? Check this chart to see out what might end up underwater.

THE STATUE OF LIBERTY 305 feet (93 m)

12 GIRAFFES 216 feet (66 m)

5 SCHOOL BUSES 200 feet (61 m)

6 ORCAS 192 feet (59 m)

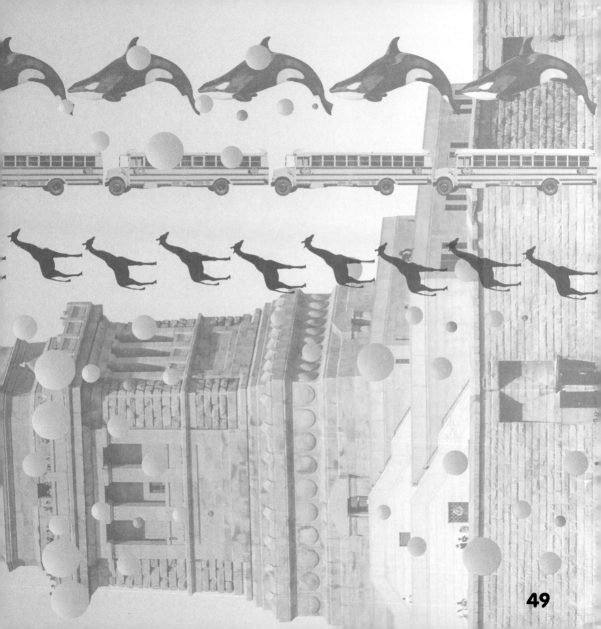

49

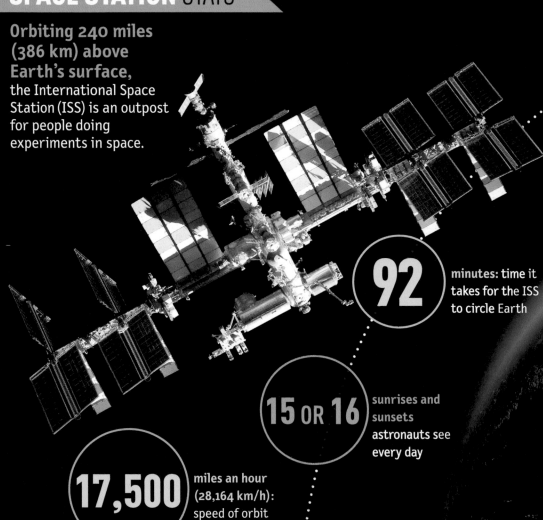

SPACE STATION STATS

Orbiting 240 miles (386 km) above Earth's surface, the International Space Station (ISS) is an outpost for people doing experiments in space.

92 minutes: time it takes for the ISS to circle Earth

15 OR 16 sunrises and sunsets astronauts see every day

17,500 miles an hour (28,164 km/h): speed of orbit

167 x 357.5 feet (51 x 109 m): size, about the same as an American football field

1,000,000 pounds (453,600 kg): total weight, heavier than 70 African elephants

SENSE OF SMELL

Pee-ew! Mammals use their sense of smell to seek out food, avoid predators, and find a mate. But some are better sniffers than others, and the mammals that reign supreme have more olfactory receptors dedicated to smelling. The amount of receptors is determined by the number of scent genes in an animal's DNA—the more you have, the better you sniff! Check out the number of genes devoted to smell in these mammals to see who takes the best whiff.

DOG
811

GUINEA PIG
796

AFRICAN ELEPHANT
1,948

RABBIT
768

ORANGUTAN
296

Some sharks can smell one drop of blood in **25 million** drops of ocean.

A polar bear can smell a seal on the ice from **20 miles** away. (32 KM)

The human brain can detect more than **10,000** different smells.

HORSE
1,066

HUMAN
396

RAT
1,207

It's sleek, energy efficient, and the longest commercial aircraft in the United States. The whole fleet of Boeing 747 planes have flown more than 5 billion people. What else makes these awesome airplanes stand out?

14
stair steps to the upper deck

2.5
MINUTES
length of time it takes the jet to travel the length of a marathon (26.2 miles/42.2 km)

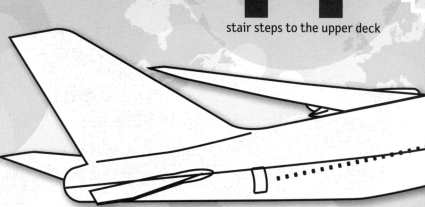

Range:
7,790 NAUTICAL MILES
(14,430 km)

This plane could fly from Miami, Florida, U.S.A., to London, United Kingdom, and back, before landing.

Fuel tank holds:

63,034 U.S. GALLONS (238,604 L)

That amount of fuel would fill the tank of over **5,000** small cars!

Length:

250 FEET, 2 INCHES
(76 m)

That's as long as a **25-story** building is tall.

1 wing can fit in the same floor space as 4 houses, each with 3 bedrooms and 2 baths.

TRASH BREAKDOWN

After you toss out a banana peel, a soda can, or a smelly sock, it's out of sight, but it's still around—sometimes for weeks, and other times for hundreds of years! Here's a timeline of how long it takes everyday trash to decompose—or completely break down—in a landfill.

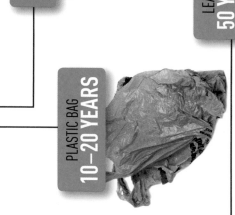

BANANA PEEL
2–5 WEEKS

APPLE CORE
2 MONTHS

WOOL SOCKS
1–5 YEARS

PLASTIC BAG
10–20 YEARS

LEATHER
50 YEARS

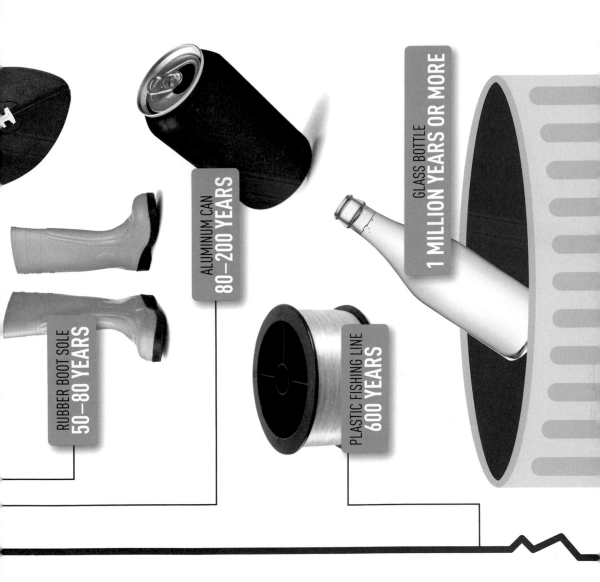

RUBBER BOOT SOLE
50–80 YEARS

ALUMINUM CAN
80–200 YEARS

PLASTIC FISHING LINE
600 YEARS

GLASS BOTTLE
1 MILLION YEARS OR MORE

BLACKBEARD'S **REVENGE**

Blackbeard was one of the most feared pirates ever to sail the ocean. From 1716 to 1718 his crew terrorized ships sailing the Atlantic Ocean and Caribbean Sea, stealing as much as they could find. The wreck of his ship, the *Queen Anne's Revenge,* was found near Beaufort, North Carolina, U.S.A., packed with awesome artifacts and cool stats.

Number of masts:

3

Length of the ship:

100 feet (30 m)

Crew of **220** pirates

Number of artifacts recovered:

280,000

Weight of anchor:

2,000 pounds (900 kg)

Length of one of the ship's anchors:

11 feet (3.4 m)

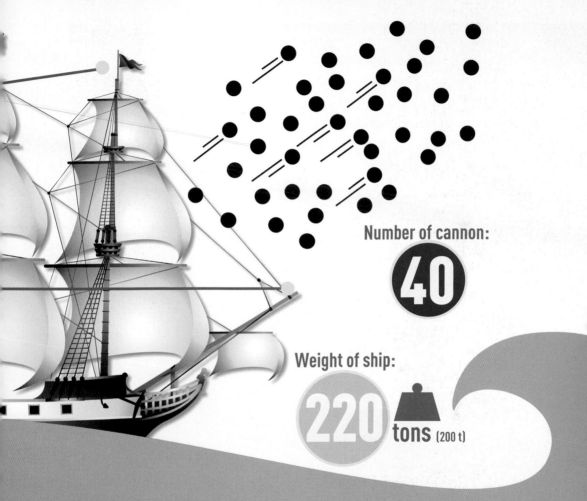

Number of cannon:

40

Weight of ship:

220 tons (200 t)

The shipwreck laid in the ocean for
almost 300 years.

Talk about busy bees! Check out all the time, energy, effort, and numbers it takes honeybees to collect nectar to make their sweet honey.

HONEYBEES COLLECT NECTAR, WHICH THEY GET FROM FLOWERS USING THEIR STRAWLIKE TONGUE. ABOUT **80%** OF NECTAR IS WATER AND **20%** IS SUGARS.

WORKER BEES CHEW ON THE NECTAR FOR **30 MINUTES,** WHICH BREAKS THE COMPLEX SUGAR IN THE NECTAR INTO SIMPLE SUGARS.

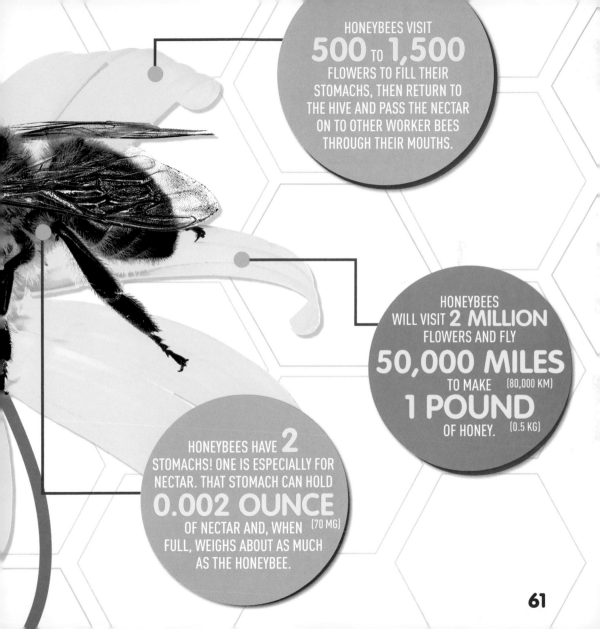

HONEYBEES VISIT
500 TO **1,500**
FLOWERS TO FILL THEIR
STOMACHS, THEN RETURN TO
THE HIVE AND PASS THE NECTAR
ON TO OTHER WORKER BEES
THROUGH THEIR MOUTHS.

HONEYBEES
WILL VISIT **2 MILLION**
FLOWERS AND FLY
50,000 MILES
TO MAKE   (80,000 KM)
1 POUND
OF HONEY.   (0.5 KG)

HONEYBEES HAVE **2**
STOMACHS! ONE IS ESPECIALLY FOR
NECTAR. THAT STOMACH CAN HOLD
0.002 OUNCE
OF NECTAR AND, WHEN   (70 MG)
FULL, WEIGHS ABOUT AS MUCH
AS THE HONEYBEE.

To outer space—and beyond!

The space race between the United States and the former Soviet Union heated up in the 1950s. See when these countries reached these out-of-this-world milestones.

MARCH 18, 1965

Soviet cosmonaut Alexei Leonov spends **10 minutes** on a space walk.

OCTOBER 4, 1957:

The U.S.S.R.* launches Sputnik 1, the first satellite in space. It weighed about **184 pounds** (84 kg) and took about **98 minutes** to orbit the Earth.

MAY 5, 1961:

Astronaut Alan Shepard becomes the first American in space, spending **15 minutes** in suborbital space.

APRIL 12, 1961:

Soviet cosmonaut Yuri Gagarin becomes the first person in space. He orbits the Earth at about **200 miles** (320 km).

FEBRUARY 20, 1962:

American astronaut John Glenn orbits the Earth **3 times** in a nearly **5-hour** flight.

*Union of Soviet Socialist Republics

JULY 30, 1971

First rover on the moon, as part of the American Apollo 15 mission. It drives 17 miles (27 km).

APRIL 12, 1981:

NASA launches the first space shuttle. It touches down, like a plane, 2 days later.

MAY 14, 1973

Skylab, the first American space station, is launched. 9 astronauts will spend time on the station from 1973 to 1974.

FEBRUARY 20, 1986:

The first section of the Soviet space station Mir is launched. It will end up having 6 docking ports.

JULY 20, 1976

The U.S. sends Viking 1, the first Mars lander, to the red planet. It was supposed to gather data for 90 days but ended up working for more than 6 years.

JULY 4, 1997:

NASA's Pathfinder probe lands on Mars. Its micro-rover weighed 22 pounds (10 kg).

JULY 20, 1969:

2 American astronauts, Neil Armstrong and 'Edwin "Buzz" Aldrin, walk on the moon.

HOW TALL IS IT?

The world's tallest building, Burj Khalifa, located in Dubai in the United Arab Emirates, soars over half a mile (0.8 km) high. But how does that compare to other cool sights around the globe? Check out this lineup to find out!

The Willis Tower has **16,100** windows.

More than **36,000** stones make up the Washington Monument.

EIFFEL TOWER **1,063** FEET (324 m)

GREAT PYRAMID **451** FEET (138 m)

WASHINGTON MONUMENT **555** FEET (169 m)

EMPIRE STATE BUILDING **1,454** FEET (443 m) (WITH ANTENNA)

WILLIS TOWER **1,730** FEET (530 m) (WITH TWIN ANTENNAS)

BURJ KHALIFA **2,717** FEET (828 m)

3,000

2,500

2,000

1,500 —

1,000 —

500

JAVANESE **2.9%**

By 2100, half of the Earth's languages may become extinct. A language dies out about every 14 days.

JAPANESE **4.3%**

RUSSIAN **5.8%**

BENGALI **6.7%**

Only 2 English words end in "gry": angry and hungry.

PORTUGUESE **7%**

ARABIC **8.3%**

HINDI **9%**

There are some 50 official languages spoken by only 1 person.

29.6% CHINESE

Speak up! There are some 7,000 languages spoken around the world today. Some people speak a few different languages, but everyone has their "first" language, the one you learned as a baby. Here are the percentages of first-language speakers for the top 10 world languages.

One study found that women and men speak about the same number of words per day—16,000.

14.5% SPANISH

11.7% ENGLISH

This chart doesn't quite add up to 100% because the numbers are rounded.

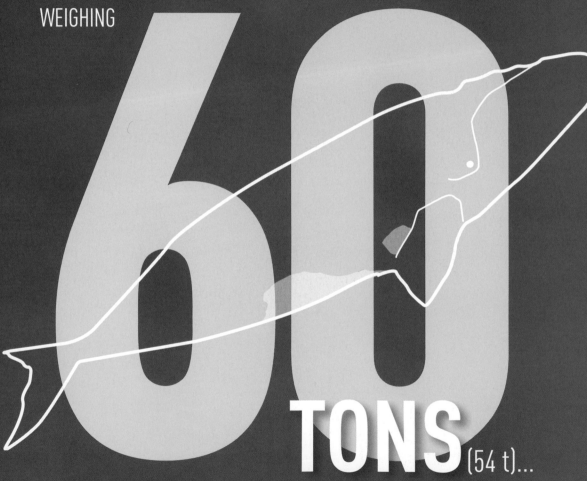

THE ENDANGERED **NORTH PACIFIC RIGHT WHALE** IS AN OCEAN TITAN, WEIGHING

60

TONS (54 t)...

THE SAME AS

34

PASSENGER CARS!

TALKING TURKEY

For many families, Thanksgiving is all about turkey, gravy, gathering around the table, and football. Here are some facts about the holiday that won't make you feel stuffed.

60' x 25' x 56'

[18 M x 7.6 M x 17 M]

DIMENSIONS OF THE "DIARY OF A WIMPY KID" BALLOON AT THE MACY'S THANKSGIVING DAY PARADE

140

APPROXIMATE NUMBER OF ENGLISH COLONISTS AND WAMPANOAG MEN AT THE FIRST THANKSGIVING IN PLYMOUTH COLONY, IN 1621

242,000,000

NUMBER OF TURKEYS RAISED IN THE U.S.A., IN 2014

316

NUMBER OF CALORIES IN A PIECE OF HOMEMADE PUMPKIN PIE

4,400

NUMBER OF CRANBERRIES IN ONE GALLON OF CRANBERRY JUICE

7,000,000

NUMBER OF WILD TURKEYS IN THE U.S.A.

71

BIG BUCKS **BLOCKBUSTERS**

Green may be the color of money, but the movie that holds the record for making the most at the box office worldwide was all about blue aliens—*Avatar.* Here are the top 10 most successful movies of all time, based on global box office revenue.

1

AVATAR
$2.78 BILLION

2

TITANIC
$2.18 BILLION

3

MARVEL'S THE AVENGERS
$1.52 BILLION

4

HARRY POTTER AND THE
DEATHLY HALLOWS—PART 2
$1.33 BILLION

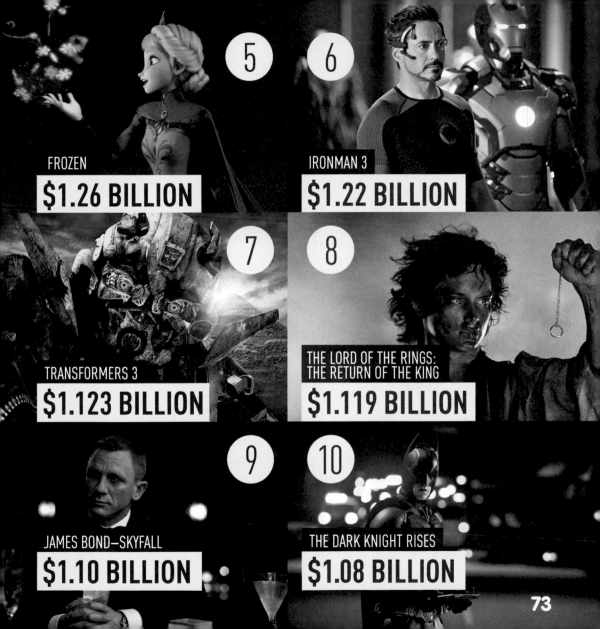

5

FROZEN

$1.26 BILLION

6

IRONMAN 3

$1.22 BILLION

7

TRANSFORMERS 3

$1.123 BILLION

8

THE LORD OF THE RINGS:
THE RETURN OF THE KING

$1.119 BILLION

9

JAMES BOND–SKYFALL

$1.10 BILLION

10

THE DARK KNIGHT RISES

$1.08 BILLION

SPILLING THE BEANS

Stop before you pop that jelly bean in your mouth!
Ever wonder how it's made? It takes from 7 to 21 days (depending on the flavor) to make a bean—and there are a lot of steps along the way!

1 INGREDIENTS FOR THE GOOEY CENTER ARE BLENDED IN A LARGE MIXER. ONE COMPANY MAKES BEANS IN MORE THAN

100

DIFFERENT FLAVORS.

2 THE MIXTURE IS POURED INTO TRAYS.

EACH TRAY HAS **1,260** BEAN-SHAPED IMPRESSIONS.

3 THE BEANS ARE COOLED OFF, THEN GIVEN A STEAM BATH AND SET ASIDE FOR

24–48 HOURS.

4 A BATCH OF **200 POUNDS** (91 KG) OF BEANS ARE PUT IN A ROTATING DRUM WHERE FOUR LAYERS OF SUGAR AND FLAVORED SYRUP ARE ADDED OVER A PERIOD OF **2 HOURS** TO BUILD UP THE SHELL.

5 A BATCH OF **400 POUNDS** (181 KG) OF BEANS ARE DROPPED IN A ROTATING DRUM WHERE GLAZE IS POURED ON THEM.

6 THE BEANS ARE SET ASIDE FOR ANOTHER **24 HOURS.**

7 THE BEANS ARE SENT OFF TO PACKAGING, THEN MOVED TO PALLETS AND SHIPPED TO STORES. THE JELLY BEAN COMPANY SHIPS BEANS TO OVER **70** COUNTRIES.

FEELING THE **BURN**

Olympic athletes are all competing for the gold, but they burn different amounts of calories to get it. Check out these popular winter sports to see how many calories a 220-pound (100-kg) elite Olympian can burn in just 10 minutes!

175 calories

ICE HOCKEY

70 calories

BOBSLED

123 calories

CURLING

245
calories

CROSS-COUNTRY SKIING

ICE DANCING

SPEED SKATING

262
calories

233
calories

The first Olympic Winter Games weren't held until **1924.**

BIG FOOTPRINT

Humans release carbon dioxide (CO_2)—a greenhouse gas—into the atmosphere when we burn fossil fuels for our electricity and transportation, or when we produce cement, metal, and steel! All countries release these gases, but who has the biggest carbon footprint? This graphic shows the 18 biggest carbon dioxide offenders and how many metric tons of carbon they release each year. How does your country rank?

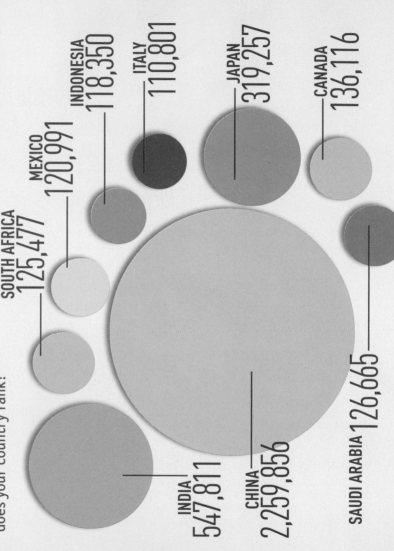

INDONESIA
118,350

ITALY
110,801

JAPAN
319,257

CANADA
136,116

MEXICO
120,991

SOUTH AFRICA
125,477

INDIA
547,811

CHINA
2,259,856

SAUDI ARABIA 126,665

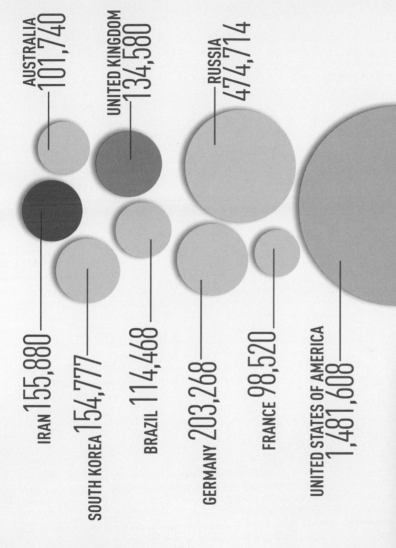

AUSTRALIA 101,740

UNITED KINGDOM 134,580

RUSSIA 474,714

IRAN 155,880

SOUTH KOREA 154,777

BRAZIL 114,468

GERMANY 203,268

FRANCE 98,520

UNITED STATES OF AMERICA 1,481,608

Plants release vapors that help cool the planet—but only counter 1 percent of global warming.

Dinosaurs dominated the Earth during the Jurassic period. No matter if they were plant-eaters or predators, they packed a punch—and these numbers prove it.

STEGOSAURUS WAS
30 FEET (9 M)
LONG—THAT'S THE LENGTH OF 2.5 SMALL CARS!

88-TON (80-t)
HEAVYWEIGHT
BRACHIOSAURUS TOWERED
52 FEET (16 M)
HIGH—THAT'S EYE TO EYE WITH 3 STACKED GIRAFFES!

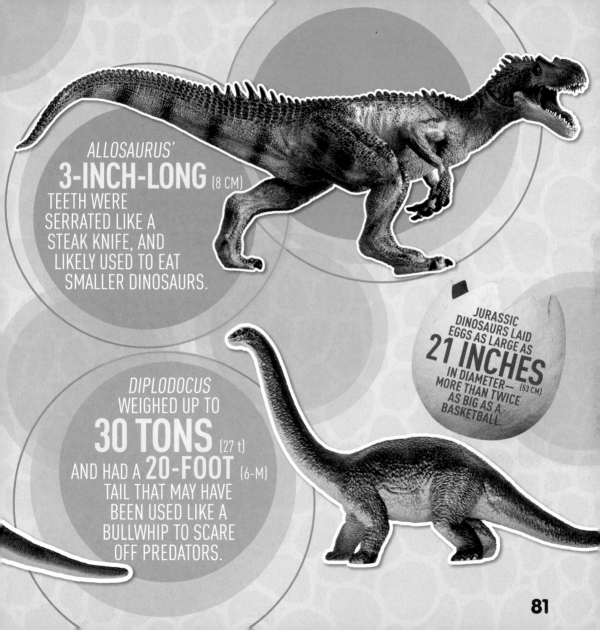

ALLOSAURUS'
3-INCH-LONG (8 CM)
TEETH WERE SERRATED LIKE A STEAK KNIFE, AND LIKELY USED TO EAT SMALLER DINOSAURS.

JURASSIC DINOSAURS LAID EGGS AS LARGE AS
21 INCHES
IN DIAMETER— (53 CM)
MORE THAN TWICE AS BIG AS A BASKETBALL.

DIPLODOCUS WEIGHED UP TO
30 TONS (27 t)
AND HAD A **20-FOOT** (6-M) TAIL THAT MAY HAVE BEEN USED LIKE A BULLWHIP TO SCARE OFF PREDATORS.

SURE, YOU SEE AND USE NUMBERS EVERY DAY, but did you

know that numbers have the power to really help people? That's what data scientist Dr. Susan Murphy is working to achieve. She and her colleagues have developed new ways to collect and process data that allows scientists to figure out which sequence of treatments can help people who are struggling with difficult diseases. Next time you're feeling stressed or overwhelmed, imagine being able to turn on your smartphone and meet "a coach"—developed with Dr. Murphy's research—that will make you feel better. That seems pretty unbelievable, right? But Dr. Murphy is working with numbers to make it happen.

WANT TO BECOME A DATA SCIENTIST?
HERE ARE DR. MURPHY'S TIPS!

1 TAKE AS MANY MATH CLASSES AS POSSIBLE SO YOU CAN FIGURE OUT WHICH MATH DISCIPLINE YOU ENJOY THE MOST.

2 ASK YOUR MATHEMATICS TEACHERS FOR ADVICE AND ALWAYS DO THE EXTRA CREDIT PROBLEM—THE MORE YOU PRACTICE, THE BETTER YOU'LL BE!

3 STRUGGLING WITH MATH PROBLEMS IN CLASS? DON'T SWEAT IT. SOMETIMES LEARNING WHERE YOU WENT WRONG HELPS THE MOST. IF YOU'RE STUCK, DON'T EVER GIVE UP. ASK FOR HELP!

PIZZA OR **FUFU?**

Your answer to the question, "What's your favorite food?" might say something about where you live. Check out the very different answers given when people in the United States and Ghana, Africa, were asked to name their favorite dish.

0.8% - BEANS

0.5% - KOKONTE

1.6% - AKPELE

0.9% - WAAKYE

0.5% - TUBAANI

2.9% - PLANTAIN

3.6% - KENKEY

6.5% - YAM

28.2% - FUFU

GHANA

6.9% - TUO ZAAFI

18.7% - BANKU

25.8% - RICE

FUFU

Americans eat an average of **46 SLICES** of pizza per year.

7.6% - OTHER

2.4% - CHOCOLATE

15.2% - PIZZA

2.4% - SUSHI/SASHIMI

2.6% - ICE CREAM

3.3% - BURGER

U.S.A.

3.6% - SEAFOOD

8.2% - STEAK

4.1% - ITALIAN

7.5% - CHICKEN

4.3% - PASTA

5.3% - MEXICAN

HERE COMES THE BABY

Just how long does it take for a baby to develop, or gestate, before it is born? It depends on the animal! Here are some average lengths for how long it takes for different animals to enter the world.

0 Days

VIRGINIA OPOSSUM
12 DAYS

WALRUS
31 DAYS

LEOPARD
94 DAYS

CHICKEN
21 DAYS

DOG
62–64 DAYS

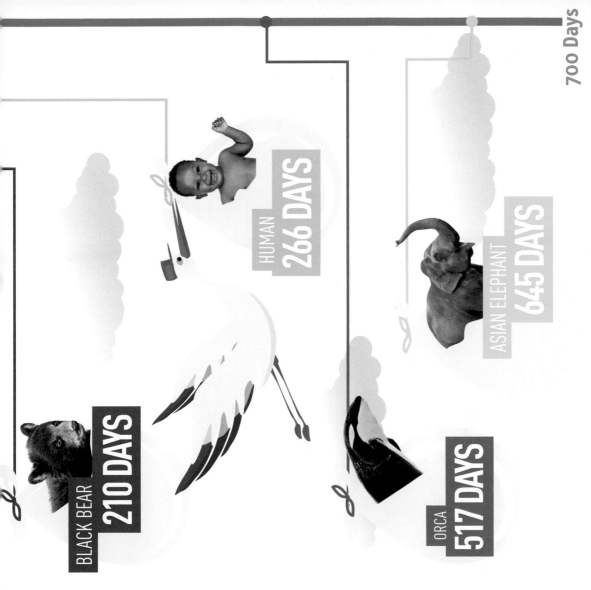

HUMAN
266 DAYS

ASIAN ELEPHANT
645 DAYS

BLACK BEAR
210 DAYS

ORCA
517 DAYS

HURRICANE HAPPENINGS

A storm is coming!
But is it a tropical cyclone, a hurricane, or a typhoon? These weather events go by different names depending on where they form and how fast their winds get. Strong tropical cyclones are called hurricanes in the Atlantic and parts of the Pacific Ocean; in the western Pacific they are called typhoons. But any way you look at it, these storms pack a punch.

1,380 MILES (2,221 km)

diameter of the most massive tropical cyclone ever recorded, 1979's Typhoon Tip

82°F (27.8°C)

water surface temperature necessary for a tropical cyclone to form

16.6

average number of tropical storms each year in the Northeast and Central Pacific Basins

12.1
average number of tropical storms in the Atlantic Basin each year

254 MPH
(408 km/h)

strongest gust of storm wind ever recorded.

12-25 MILES
(20-40 km)

diameter of a hurricane eye

31
number of days Hurricane John lasted in 1994

10
number of Hurricane Sandy—related pictures uploaded every second to Instagram on October 29, 2012

GREAT PYRAMID, GREAT NUMBERS

More than 4,500 years ago, Pharaoh Khufu began building what would become the Earth's biggest pyramid. Since pharaohs expected to become gods in the afterlife, they created massive pyramid tombs inside the pyramids—filling them with things they would need to guide and sustain them in the next world. See how the numbers on the Great Pyramid stack up.

WEIGHT OF LARGEST STONE BLOCKS:
15 TONS
(14 t)

NUMBER OF STONE BLOCKS:
2.3 MILLION

AVERAGE LENGTH OF EACH SIDE:
756 FEET
(230 M)

NUMBER OF BUILDERS:  20,000

Its sides are accurately oriented to the **4 points** of the compass.

HEIGHT: **451 FEET** (138 M)

DUE TO EROSION, THE PYRAMID IS **30 FEET** (9 M) SHORTER THAN IT WAS ORIGINALLY.

ANGLE AT WHICH THE SIDES RISE: **51°52″**

SCREAM FOR **HALLOWEEN**

The holiday for ghosts and ghouls rolls around every October 31. Check out these spooky numerical facts about All Hallow's Eve—they might just surprise you.

2,009 POUNDS
[911.3 KG]

WEIGHT OF THE LARGEST PUMPKIN EVER GROWN

500

AVERAGE NUMBER OF SEEDS IN A PUMPKIN

1,333

NUMBER OF BUSINESSES PRODUCING CHOCOLATE AND COCOA PRODUCTS IN THE U.S.

24

NUMBER OF COLORS YOU CAN FIND IN M&MS

252 NUMBER OF LICKS TO GET TO THE CENTER OF A TOOTSIE POP

4,200,000 NUMBER OF TRICK-OR-TREATING-AGE KIDS ACROSS THE U.S. (CHILDREN AGES 5 TO 14)

1.2 BILLION POUNDS (544.3 MILLION KG)

WEIGHT OF ALL THE PUMPKINS GROWN IN THE U.S.

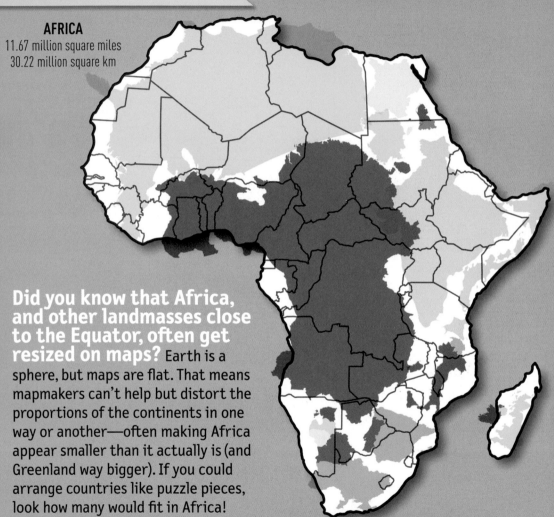

HOW BIG IS **AFRICA?**

AFRICA
11.67 million square miles
30.22 million square km

Did you know that Africa, and other landmasses close to the Equator, often get resized on maps? Earth is a sphere, but maps are flat. That means mapmakers can't help but distort the proportions of the continents in one way or another—often making Africa appear smaller than it actually is (and Greenland way bigger). If you could arrange countries like puzzle pieces, look how many would fit in Africa!

94

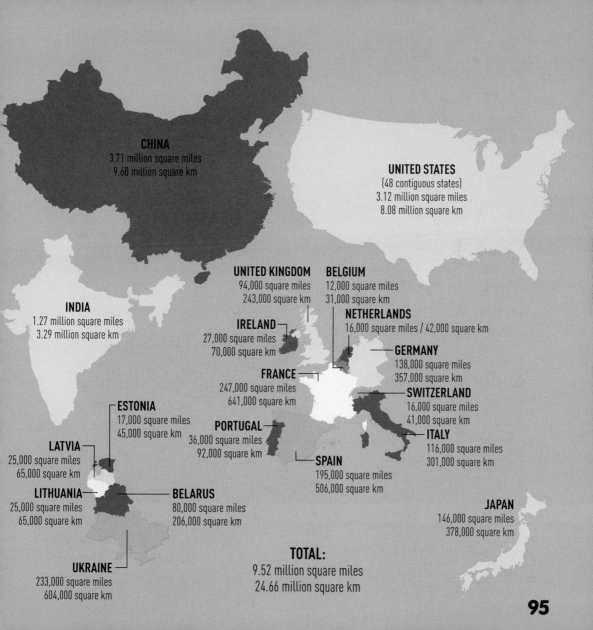

CHINA
3.71 million square miles
9.60 million square km

UNITED STATES
(48 contiguous states)
3.12 million square miles
8.08 million square km

INDIA
1.27 million square miles
3.29 million square km

UNITED KINGDOM
94,000 square miles
243,000 square km

BELGIUM
12,000 square miles
31,000 square km

IRELAND
27,000 square miles
70,000 square km

NETHERLANDS
16,000 square miles / 42,000 square km

GERMANY
138,000 square miles
357,000 square km

FRANCE
247,000 square miles
641,000 square km

SWITZERLAND
16,000 square miles
41,000 square km

ESTONIA
17,000 square miles
45,000 square km

PORTUGAL
36,000 square miles
92,000 square km

ITALY
116,000 square miles
301,000 square km

LATVIA
25,000 square miles
65,000 square km

SPAIN
195,000 square miles
506,000 square km

LITHUANIA
25,000 square miles
65,000 square km

BELARUS
80,000 square miles
206,000 square km

JAPAN
146,000 square miles
378,000 square km

UKRAINE
233,000 square miles
604,000 square km

TOTAL:
9.52 million square miles
24.66 million square km

95

GERM SHOWDOWN

Scientists in Wales studied 3 greeting styles to determine which was the cleanest. Find out which one has the upper hand.

HANDSHAKE

AN AVERAGE HANDSHAKE TRANSFERRED **MORE THAN 5 TIMES AS MUCH BACTERIA** AS A FIST BUMP. (A STRONG HANDSHAKE TRANSFERRED **10 TIMES** AS MUCH.)

HIGH FIVE

A HIGH FIVE PASSED **TWICE AS MANY** GERMS AS A FIST BUMP.

FIST BUMP

WINNER:

FIST BUMPS HAVE THE **LEAST SKIN-TO-SKIN CONTACT** OF THE GREETINGS, WHICH MAKES IT LESS LIKELY FOR MICROBES TO JUMP **FROM ONE HAND TO ANOTHER.**

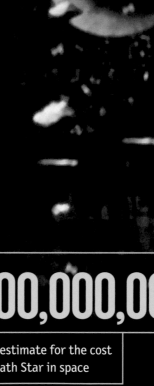

SCI-FI FACTORS

Star Wars' infamous Death Star was both a moon-size battle station and a superlaser, capable of destroying a planet. Some economists—and Star Wars fans—have wondered: Could a real Death Star be built? And at what cost? Hint: The total theater gross for all the Star Wars movies was $2.2 billion, and that would be just a drop in the bucket!

34,000

Number of people who in 2012 petitioned the U.S. government to build a real Death Star by 2016

$852,000,000,000,000,000

$852 quadrillion: How much economists estimate for the cost of materials needed to build an actual Death Star in space

833,315 years

Time it would take, at today's production rates, to make all the steel needed to produce a Death Star

2,000,000

The number of Death Stars that could be built using iron from the Earth's crust

Once completed, the most powerful laser in the world—nicknamed the Death Star—will be

100,000

times more powerful than all the power plants in the world, but that power will only be released for a fraction of a second.

A Boba Fett action figure that originally sold for $2.25 when it was made 35 years ago was recently sold at auction for $26,720.

One of Saturn's moons, Mimas, is nicknamed the Death Star because a huge crater on it makes it look like the famous battle station.

NUMBER CASCADE

Victoria Falls, fed by the Zambezi River and located on the border of Zambia and Zimbabwe, is one of Africa's most famous and natural wonders and one of the most impressive waterfalls found on Earth. Explore some of the amazing stats behind this thunderous wall of water, which has shaped the land, and ecosystem for millions of years.

354
FEET HIGH
[108 M]

142.7
BILLION GALLONS
[540 billion L]

of water drop over the falls per minute when the river is in full flood

5,538 FEET WIDE (1,688 M)

12 MILES (20 KM) distance mist can be seen for

1.25 MILES (2 KM) width of Zambezi River at the falls

0.3 MILES HIGH (500 M) maximum height of the spray plume

2,000,000 YEARS AGO time when the falls started to form

3,000,000 YEARS OLD age of stone artifacts made by early humans found near the falls

SEA OTTER STATS

Sea otters are the world's smallest marine mammals,
but there is nothing small about the numbers on these furry creatures.

SEA OTTERS EAT **25%** OF THEIR WEIGHT IN FOOD EACH DAY.

THEY CAN DIVE UP TO **300 FEET** (90 M) WHEN FORAGING FOR FOOD, SUCH AS CLAMS AND ABALONE, ON THE OCEAN FLOOR.

MALES WEIGH UP TO **65 POUNDS** (29 KG) —ABOUT THE SAME AS A GOLDEN RETRIEVER.

FEMALES GENERALLY JUST HAVE **1 PUP**, BUT SOMETIMES HAVE TWINS.

A SEA OTTER'S COAT HAS UP TO **1 MILLION** HAIRS PER SQUARE INCH—THE THICKEST FUR OF ANY MAMMAL! (YOU HAVE ONLY ABOUT **100,000 HAIRS** ON YOUR HEAD.)

A SEA OTTER'S FUR HAS **2 LAYERS**—AN UNDERCOAT AND LONGER GUARD HAIRS. THIS TRAPS A LAYER OF AIR NEXT TO THEIR SKIN SO THEIR SKIN DOESN'T GET WET!

A NEWBORN OTTER'S FUR TRAPS SO MUCH AIR IT CAN'T SINK! IT BOBS ON THE SURFACE FOR ITS FIRST **4 WEEKS**, THEN IT LEARNS TO SWIM.

4 FEET (1.2 M) LONG—ABOUT THE SIZE OF AN 8-YEAR-OLD KID.

COUNTING UP **THE COLOSSEUM**

Rome's Colosseum was built to impress.
It was the largest amphitheater in the Roman world—and its numbers still measure up. Let the games begin!

The arena was surrounded by an

18-foot (5-m)

high wall to protect spectators from being attacked by wild beasts.

The Colosseum could hold

50,000

spectators.

When the Colosseum opened in A.D. 80, there were

100 days

of games to celebrate.

It took less than **10 years** to build the

620-by-513-foot

(189 by 156 m)

Colosseum, which was ellipse-shaped to give everyone the best view possible.

Sailors raised and lowered

240

wooden masts connected to long strips of fabriclike sails on a ship to provide shade over the amphitheater.

Beneath the Colosseum, animals and gladiators stayed in

32 cages

waiting to be hoisted up into the performance area.

ANGLE OF FIRST DROP

60°

AVERAGE LENGTH OF RIDE:

18 SECONDS

STEPS TO THE TOP

264

• VERRÜCKT IS 17 STORIES TALL—THAT'S BIGGER THAN NIAGARA FALLS!

INSANE WATERSLIDE

Located in Kansas City, Kansas, U.S.A., the Verrückt—which means "insane" in German—looks like a roller coaster, but it's really the world's tallest waterslide!

HEIGHT

168 FEET, 7 INCHES (51 M)

HEIGHT

50 FEET (15 M)

NUMBER OF PEOPLE PER RAFT

1 2 3

3

• RIDERS ON THE WATERSLIDE GO FROM 5 G'S TO WEIGHTLESSNESS.

IS BIGFOOT REAL?

A hairy, monstrous, forest creature? Or a misunderstood bear? A recent survey showed that nearly 30 percent of adult Americans think Bigfoot—also known as Sasquatch—is at least "probably real."

NOT SURE

DEFINITELY REAL

10%

7%

PROBABLY REAL

22%

23%

DEFINITELY NOT REAL

38%

PROBABLY NOT REAL

California has 2 Bigfoot museums.

Bigfoot enthusiasts say the furry creature stands between 6.5 and 10 feet (2–3 m) tall and his footprint is up to 22 inches (56 cm) long.

IS THE **LOCH NESS MONSTER** REAL?

Brits are less sure about the reality of the Loch Ness Monster—the legendary creature said to inhabit Scotland's Loch Ness. What do you believe? Find out where you fall on the scale.

Some 300,000 people visit Loch Ness every year to scan the waters for Nessie.

DEFINITELY REAL
3%

NOT SURE
8%

PROBABLY REAL
14%

DEFINITELY NOT REAL
33%

PROBABLY NOT REAL
41%

Stories of a long-necked aquatic animal have been told in the Scottish Highlands for 1,500 years.

HEATING UP

The fact that our bodies automatically regulate our internal temperature is what makes us warm-blooded. But while mammals and birds are warm-blooded, normal body temperatures aren't all the same—they fall into a range. For instance, in humans, some people's body temperatures are naturally a little warmer or cooler than others. But who runs the hottest? Check out this graph to see the upper end of these animals' temperature ranges!

camel
105.8° F
(41°C)

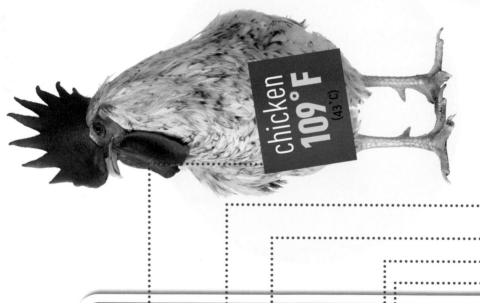

chicken
109° F
(43°C)

ANT ANTICS

Chomp chomp! These tropical insects from the Americas are known as leaf-cutter ants. These tiny creatures travel through the rain forest in groups of hundreds of thousands of ants in lines up to 100 feet (30 m) long. When these ants find their plant prey, they use their teeth to cut off pieces of leaves. But leaf-cutter ants don't eat the foliage. They march the leaves back to their nests and wait for fungi to grow on them. Then the ants eat the fungi. **Delicious!**

ANTS HAVE BEEN LIVING **ON EARTH** FOR MORE THAN **140 MILLION** YEARS.

LEAF-CUTTER NESTS CAN HAVE MORE THAN **1,000** CHAMBERS.

LEAF-CUTTERS ARE **PICKY EATERS!** ONE SPECIES FROM COSTA RICA ATE ONLY 17 OUT OF **332** PLANTS AVAILABLE TO THEM.

THESE ANTS CAN **CARRY** 50 TIMES THEIR BODY WEIGHT.

LENGTH OF ANT TRAILS: 100 FEET. (30 M)

There are a total of 39 different species of leaf-cutter ant.

LENGTH: 0.5 INCH (1.3 cm) EXCEPT FOR THE QUEEN, WHICH CAN BE MORE THAN 1 INCH LONG. (2.5 cm)

THEIR JAWS CAN **VIBRATE** 1,000 TIMES PER SECOND.

The universe may seem infinite and full of, well, space, but it's actually made up of different things—some of which we can't even see. Scientists know that the universe is made of matter you can touch (atoms), dark matter, which is matter we can't detect, and dark energy, a force that repels gravity. Here's how the universe breaks down.

DARK ENERGY - **68.3%**

Scientists were shocked when they discovered the existence of dark energy in the 1990s. But Albert Einstein may have actually included dark matter in one of his theories.

Dark matter is invisible.

The visible universe—such as stars and galaxies— is made of atoms and is also called baryonic matter.

DARK MATTER - **26.8%**

ATOMS - **4.9%**

ANIMAL SMARTS

Just how do we measure intelligence?

Can your cat remember where you left a tasty treat? Are chimps able to count? You might think that the bigger a creature's brain, the smarter it is. But don't let size fool you. Check out the stats below on some of our planet's smartest animals.

Some chimpanzees in captivity have learned up to 350 signs in American Sign Language.

CHIMPANZEE

BRAIN WEIGHT: **1 POUND** (0.6 KG)

WEIGHT: **70–130 POUNDS** (32–60 KG)

SIZE: **4–5 FEET** (3–4.2 M)

By its first birthday, a dolphin chooses a "signature whistle" that functions as its name.

BOTTLENOSE DOLPHIN

BRAIN WEIGHT: **3.5 POUNDS** (1.6 KG)

WEIGHT: **1,100 POUNDS** (500 KG)

SIZE: **10–14 FEET** (3–4.2 M)

Many elephants return to the same watering holes year after year. They even remember how to get there, even when the water is hundreds of miles (km) away.

10-YEAR-OLD BOY

BRAIN WEIGHT: **3 POUNDS** (1.4 KG)

WEIGHT: **82 POUNDS** (37 KG)

SIZE: **55 INCHES** (1.4 M)

AFRICAN ELEPHANT

BRAIN WEIGHT: **10.5 POUNDS** (4.8 KG)

WEIGHT: **5,000–14,000 POUNDS** (2,268–6,350 KG)

SIZE: **8.2–13 FEET** (2.5–4 M) AT THE SHOULDER

Cats hear us call, and they recognize our voice. When they don't come, it's because they're ignoring us.

NEW CALEDONIAN CROW

BRAIN WEIGHT: **0.02 POUND** (7.6 G)

WEIGHT: **0.6 POUND** (277 G)

SIZE: **12 INCHES** (30.5 CM)

New Caledonian crows will use 3 different tools to reach 1 scrap of meat.

CAT

BRAIN WEIGHT: **0.07 POUND** (30 g)

WEIGHT: **5–20 POUNDS** (2.3–9 KG)

SIZE: **28 INCHES** (71 CM)

Scientists say dogs are 4 times more likely to take your food when they think you're not looking.

DOG (BEAGLE)

BRAIN WEIGHT: **0.16 POUND** (0.07 KG)

WEIGHT: **20–25 POUNDS** (9–11 KG)

SIZE: **15 INCHES** (38 CM) AT THE SHOULDER

Bags packed and ready to ride ... or fly ... or drive!

When people travel to a different country, do they race through an airport boarding gate or hop in a car? Find out the most popular ways to jet off to an international destination.

53%

AIR

Airplanes today are **75 percent** quieter than those built **50** years ago.

40% ROAD

2% RAIL

5% WATER

HOMETOWN **HOOPS**

Want to go pro someday?

All professional basketball players were once just young kids shooting hoops on local courts. For players from the U.S., see the numbers behind where NBA players on 2014 rosters were born.

CALIFORNIA
59

NEW YORK
24

ILLINOIS
16

MARYLAND
10

WASHINGTON
15

OHIO
12

ARKANSAS
4

WISCONSIN
5

MISSISSIPPI
7

MINNESOTA
6

OREGON
3

ALABAMA
4

COLORADO
1

ARIZONA
2

NEW MEXICO
3

WYOMING
1

CONNECTICUT
9

NEW HAMPSHIRE
1

FLORIDA
16

TEXAS
21

NEW JERSEY
9

LOUISIANA
12

INDIANA
16

PENNSYLVANIA
13

MICHIGAN
12

GEORGIA
9

MISSOURI
9

N. CAROLINA
10

S. CAROLINA
7

TENNESSEE
10

IOWA
3

KENTUCKY
3

MASS.
4

VIRGINIA
5

OKLAHOMA
2

W. VIRGINIA
2

NEVADA
1

RHODE ISLAND
1

S. DAKOTA
1

ALASKA
1

N. DAKOTA
1

TWISTER TOTALS

The United States has more tornadoes than any other country, with an average of about

1,200

recorded each year. Florida and "Tornado Alley" in the south-central U.S. have the highest rate of twisters. Check out this map of the average number of tornadoes in each state to see how yours measures up.

20

19

28

21

18

36

35

1

2

2

5

3

0

36

27

23

16

10

3

1

1

36

27

10

10

6

3

47

21

10

12

14

137

26

23

21

10

27

52

A British chocolatier created a candy box with more than **220,000** chocolates in it.

SWITZERLAND
12.7 POUNDS
(5.8 kg)

BELGIUM
12.5 POUNDS
(5.7 kg)

GERMANY
8 POUNDS
(4 kg)

UNITED KINGDOM
7.8 POUNDS
(3.5 kg)

THE SWEETEST COUNTRIES

Hershey's Kisses have been around for more than
100 YEARS.

Think you have a sweet tooth?
Well, you're not alone. The world eats 4.1 million tons (3.7 million t) of chocolate every year. So which country has an especially sweet spot for chocolate? Check out the average amount of cocoa eaten by people around the world to find out!

In the United States,
1,379
different plants manufacture chocolate products.

UNITED STATES
5.4 POUNDS
(2.5 kg)

SWEDEN
5 POUNDS
(2 kg)

JAPAN
2.8 POUNDS
(1.3 kg)

BRAZIL
2 POUNDS
(1 kg)

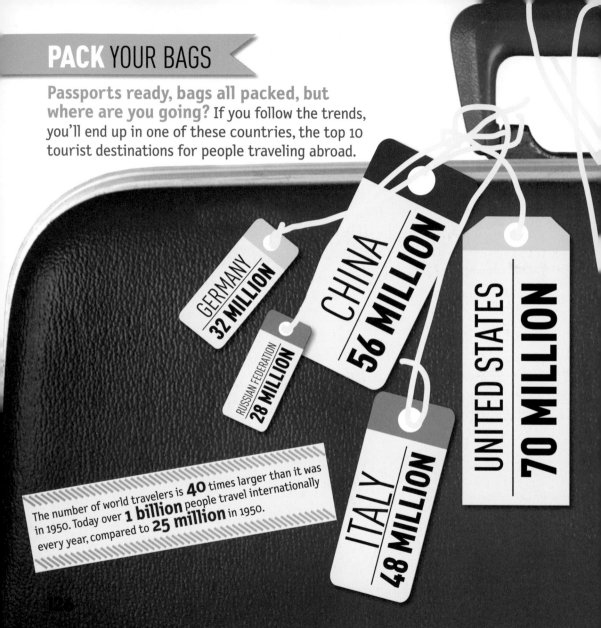

PACK YOUR BAGS

Passports ready, bags all packed, but **where are you going?** If you follow the trends, you'll end up in one of these countries, the top 10 tourist destinations for people traveling abroad.

GERMANY
32 MILLION

RUSSIAN FEDERATION
28 MILLION

CHINA
56 MILLION

UNITED STATES
70 MILLION

ITALY
48 MILLION

The number of world travelers is **40** times larger than it was in 1950. Today over **1 billion** people travel internationally every year, compared to **25 million** in 1950.

FRANCE
83 MILLION

SPAIN
61 MILLION

TURKEY
38 MILLION

UNITED KINGDOM
31 MILLION

THAILAND
27 MILLION

01588

CHECKPOINT CHARLIE
BERLIN

A SPACE CALLED HOME

Far out! Though space travel and science advance every day, some people aren't so sure we'll be living out there someday. A poll of adult Americans asked: Will humans build colonies on another planet that can be lived in for long periods of time? Here's how they answered:

PROBABLY NOT

39%

A space suit weighs **280 pounds** (127 kg) on Earth.

28% PROBABLY

5% DEFINITELY

3% DON'T KNOW

25% DEFINITELY NOT

ADMIT ONE

SPACE

$250,000

One private company plans to take tourists on a 2-hour flight into space for **$250,000** a ticket.

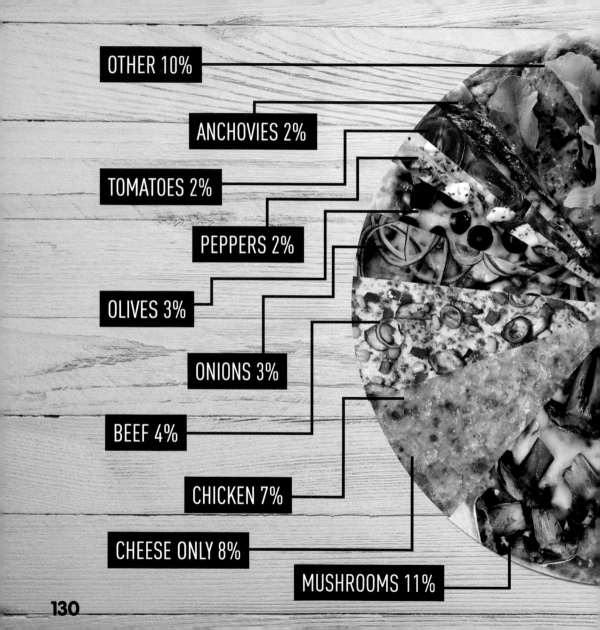

OTHER 10%

ANCHOVIES 2%

TOMATOES 2%

PEPPERS 2%

OLIVES 3%

ONIONS 3%

BEEF 4%

CHICKEN 7%

CHEESE ONLY 8%

MUSHROOMS 11%

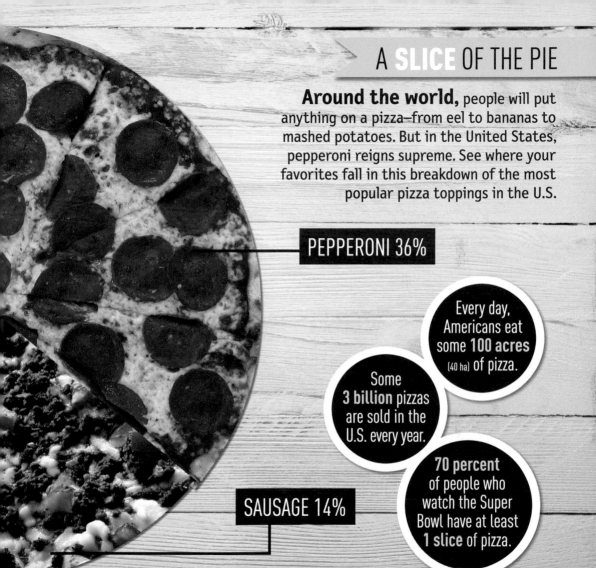

A **SLICE** OF THE PIE

Around the world, people will put anything on a pizza—from eel to bananas to mashed potatoes. But in the United States, pepperoni reigns supreme. See where your favorites fall in this breakdown of the most popular pizza toppings in the U.S.

PEPPERONI 36%

Every day, Americans eat some **100 acres** (40 ha) of pizza.

Some **3 billion** pizzas are sold in the U.S. every year.

SAUSAGE 14%

70 percent of people who watch the Super Bowl have at least **1 slice** of pizza.

PLANETARY SMACKDOWN

One is the largest planet in our solar system (by far!), so large that more than 1,000 Earths would fit inside. The other is a dwarf planet orbiting at the very edge of our solar system, so distant that scientists can't even see it clearly. But which one is more extreme? You decide.

NAMED AFTER GREEK GODDESS OF STRIFE AND DISCORD

MADE OF ROCK WITH SURFACE OF NITROGEN AND METHANE ICE

LENGTH OF ORBIT **557** EARTH YEARS

POSITION FROM SUN IN ORBIT **13TH**

KNOWN MOONS **1**

ERIS

LENGTH OF DAY **25.5** EARTH HOURS

SURFACE TEMPERATURES **-359°F** TO **-405°F** (-217°C to -243°C)

CLOSEST ORBIT TO SUN **3,582,660,264** MILES (5,765,732,799 KM)

JUPITER

NAMED AFTER	ROMAN KING OF THE GODS
MADE OF	GAS LAYERS OF **HYDROGEN AND HELIUM** AND LIQUID LAYER OF **METALLIC HYDROGEN,** POSSIBLY A SOLID CORE
LENGTH OF ORBIT	**12** EARTH YEARS
POSITION FROM SUN IN ORBIT	**6TH**
KNOWN MOONS	**67**
LENGTH OF DAY	**9.9** EARTH HOURS
SURFACE TEMPERATURES	**-234˚F** (-148˚C)
CLOSEST ORBIT TO SUN	**460,237,112** MILES (740,679,835 KM)

All of the asteroids in the asteroid belt could easily fit inside of Eris.

Five dwarf planets have been found so far in our solar system, but astronomers think there may be **100** or more.

Jupiter's moon Europa has an ice-covered ocean. It is salty like those on Earth, but almost **10 times** deeper.

RAIN FOREST FIGURES

Rain forests around the world are places of record-setting diversity. Even though they cover less than 2 percent of Earth's surface, they are home to half of the planet's plants and animals. See how rain forests measure up.

WINGSPAN OF QUEEN ALEXANDRA'S BIRDWING BUTTERFLY:

12 INCHES [31 CM]

THE WEIGHT OF AFRICA'S GOLIATH BEETLE IS

3.5 OUNCES. [100 G]

THAT'S AS MUCH AS A SMALL APPLE!

MACAWS OFTEN GATHER IN GROUPS OF

10–30 BIRDS,

THEIR LOUD SQUAWKS ECHOING THROUGH THE CANOPY.

EVERY

SECOND

AN AREA OF RAIN FOREST THE SIZE OF A FOOTBALL FIELD IS CLEARED FOR CROPS, PASTURES, WOOD, FUEL, AND ROADS.

1 IN 4

OF THE INGREDIENTS IN MEDICINE ARE MADE FROM RAIN FOREST PLANTS.

TOUCANS USE THEIR

7.5-INCH [19-cm]

BILL TO SNATCH HARD-TO-REACH FRUIT!

20% OF THE WORLD'S FRESH WATER IS IN THE AMAZON BASIN.

ONLY ABOUT

2 INCHES [5 cm]

LONG, THE RED-EYED TREE FROG HIDES IN THE RAIN FOREST CANOPY AND SNAGS PREY WITH ITS STICKY TONGUE.

29 FEET [9 m].

RAIN FOREST–DWELLING GREEN ANACONDAS, THE LARGEST SNAKES IN THE WORLD, CAN GROW TO MORE THAN

135

HOW DOES A SCIENTIST COLLECT DATA AND SHARE IT WITH THE WORLD?

MEET >>

HILARY MASON GIVES US THE INSIDE SCOOP:

FIRST

I gather data. Usually this data is from people using the Internet, and I collect it by programming software to store and clean it.

NEXT

I develop a mathematical way of looking at that data. For example, let's say we have a thermometer measuring temperature. I look at the behavior of the temperature— things like average and highest and lowest values—and I ask questions. For example, why is the temperature getting hotter each day?

HILARY MASON, COMPUTER SCIENTIST

THEN

We learn something great. Maybe the temperature outside is going up each day because winter is about to transition into spring! As a data scientist, I get to play with a bunch of different ways of asking questions and looking at the data in order to figure out new things about our world.

FINALLY

I can make a chart or a graph or tell a story to share everything I have learned with other people. Great data scientists have to be creative in order to ask good questions and figure out how to answer them clearly and technically.

How long does it take to travel the 350 miles (560 km) between San Francisco and Los Angeles, California, U.S.A.? It depends on your mode of transportation. Billionaire inventor Elon Musk hopes to some day make a solar-powered vehicle called the "Hyperloop" — where people could zip between the 2 cities in the time it takes to eat dinner.

8 DAYS

WALKING

Assuming 3 miles an hour (5 km/h) for 14 hours per day

37 MINUTES

AIRPLANE

Assuming a speed of 570 miles an hour (920 km/h)

Redwood National Park

Yosemite National Park

Golden Gate Bridge

San Francisco

Mojave Desert

Joshua Tree National Park

Los Angeles
Disneyland

28
MINUTES
HYPERLOOP
Assuming a speed of 760 miles an hour (1,220 km/h)

6.4 HOURS
Assuming a speed of 55 miles an hour (90 km/h)

CAR

If you could drive a car to the moon, it would take you **167 days** to get there, driving 60 miles an hour (97 km/h), 24 hours a day.

In your lifetime, you will walk about **115,000 miles** (185,075 km)— that's enough to circle the globe over 4 times!

HIT THE **BOOKS**

Got a minute?
If you spend a little time reading each day, by the time you reach high school you'll be a reading wizard. Check out how many times you can read *Harry Potter and the Sorcerer's Stone* if you read a little—or a lot—every day.

IF YOU READ
1 HOUR EVERY DAY:

EVERY YEAR, A SIXTH GRADER WILL HAVE READ: **3,285,000** words

THAT'S THE SAME AS READING *HARRY POTTER AND THE SORCERER'S STONE*: **42** times

FROM KINDERGARTEN THROUGH HIGH SCHOOL GRADUATION, YOU'LL HAVE READ FOR NEARLY: **198** days

 IF YOU READ
20 MINUTES EVERY DAY:

EVERY YEAR, A SIXTH GRADER WHO READS 20 MINUTES A DAY WILL HAVE READ: **1,095,000** words

THAT'S THE SAME AS READING *HARRY POTTER AND THE SORCERER'S STONE:* **14 times**

FROM KINDERGARTEN THROUGH HIGH SCHOOL GRADUATION, YOU'LL HAVE READ FOR: **66 days**

 IF YOU READ
5 MINUTES EVERY DAY:

The U.S. Library of Congress has some 838 miles (1,349 km) of bookshelves.

EVERY YEAR, A SIXTH GRADER WHO READS 5 MINUTES A DAY WILL READ: **273,750** words

THAT'S THE SAME AS READING *HARRY POTTER AND THE SORCERER'S STONE:* **3.5 times**

FROM KINDERGARTEN THROUGH HIGH SCHOOL GRADUATION, YOU'LL HAVE READ FOR: **14 days**

HOW **LOUD** IS IT?

Of course fireworks

on the Fourth of July are louder than a quiet library, but how much louder? Sound is measured in decibels (dB). So cover your ears and take a look at how these noises compare.

190dB
BLUE WHALE

150dB
FIREWORKS

140dB
JET ENGINE

130dB JACKHAMMER

114 dB AFRICAN LION'S ROAR

90 dB BLENDER

70 dB ALARM CLOCK

60 dB NORMAL SPEECH

40 dB NEIGHBORHOOD AT NIGHT

30 dB LIBRARY

0 dB

Measuring sound is a little tricky. In mathematics, it's measured on what's called a logarithmic scale. Earthquake strength and light intensity are a couple of other things measured this way. It works like this: Almost complete silence is 0 dB, and a sound 10 times more powerful is 10 dB. But a sound 100 times more powerful is 20 dB (an increase of 10 is a tenfold increase in sound).

BEHIND **THE BILLIONS**

7 billion people live on Earth.
That sounds like a pretty big number, but just how big is it? Let's try to put it in perspective.

Standing shoulder to shoulder, all **7 BILLION** of us could fit in the city of Los Angeles, California, U.S.A.

It would take
200 YEARS
to count to **7 BILLION** out loud.

It would take nearly 3 Olympic-size swimming pools to hold **7 BILLION** M&Ms.

If you took **7 BILLION** steps, you'd circle the globe **133 TIMES.**

If you were to stack **7 BILLION** people, that tower could reach to the moon 27 times.

LION

7 BILLION seconds =
222 YEARS

GIANTS OF THE DEEP

Some of the world's largest animals live in the ocean—gentle blue whales, gliding manta rays, mysterious giant squid. But just how big can some of these animals get? Some sea life is tough to spot, rare, or in parts of the ocean that are hard to reach. But here are the figures on some of the largest marine species ever discovered.

ADULT HUMAN

6 FEET (1.8 m)

JAPANESE SPIDER CRAB

12.1 FEET (6.9 m)
(LEG SPAN)

GIANT PACIFIC OCTOPUS

32.2 FEET (9.8 m)
(RADIAL SPREAD)

GIANT ISOPOD

1.6 FEET (9.8 m)
(TOTAL LENGTH)

LEATHERBACK SEA TURTLE

7 FEET (1.8 m)
(SHELL LENGTH)

WHALE SHARK

61.7 FEET (19 m)
(TOTAL LENGTH)

SPERM WHALE

78.7 FEET (24 m)
(TOTAL LENGTH)

GIANT SQUID

39.4 FEET (12 m)
(TOTAL LENGTH)

OARFISH

26.3 FEET (8 m)
(TOTAL LENGTH)

GIANT OCEAN MANTA RAY

23 FEET (7 m)
(DISK WIDTH)

SOUTHERN ELEPHANT SEAL

22.5 FEET (6.9 m)
(TOTAL LENGTH)

GIANT TUBE WORM

9.8 FEET (3 m)
(TUBE LENGTH)

GIANT CLAM

4.5 FEET (1.4 m)
(SHELL LENGTH)

BLUE WHALE

108.3 FEET (33 m)
(TOTAL LENGTH)

CARIBBEAN GIANT BARREL SPONGE **8.2** FEET (2.5 m)
(BASE DIAMETER)

What can you do in 6 minutes? Get ready for bed? Answer a homework question? These competitive eaters took just 6 minutes to pack away a ton of food. Check out the winning numbers behind these food champions' meals.

Joey Chestnut gorged on

121

Twinkies.

Marcos Owens stuffed himself with

34

large cannoli.

Joey Chestnut ate

15

pints [7 L] vanilla ice cream.

Patrick Bertoletti devoured

72

cupcakes.

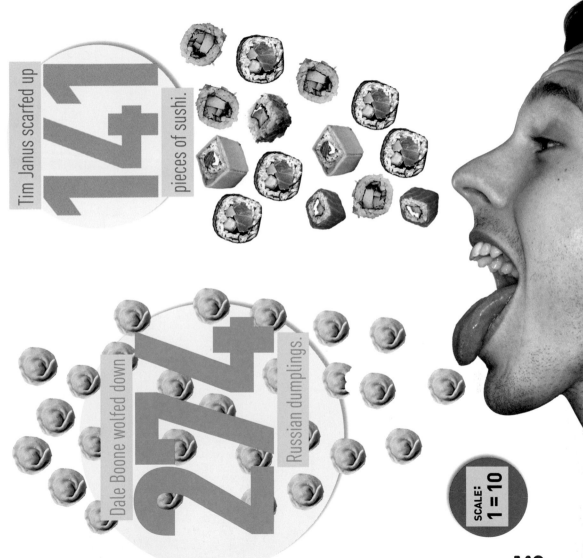

Tim Janus scarfed up **141** pieces of sushi.

Dale Boone wolfed down **274** Russian dumplings.

SCALE: 1 = 10

149

The 1939 film *The Wizard of Oz*, may be filled with songs, wicked witches, munchkins, and a pair of ruby slippers, but it's also chock-full of numbers. And you don't have to go over the rainbow to find them.

16 YEARS OLD

age of actress Judy Garland, who played Dorothy, when she filmed the movie

9 CAMERAS

hidden in plants and bushes were used to shoot some scenes of the movie.

35 FEET (11 M)

size of stockings used to make the tornado that sent Dorothy careening from Kansas to Oz

90 POUNDS (41 kg)
weight of the Cowardly Lion's costume

1,000 COSTUMES WERE USED FOR **600** ACTORS

17 YEARS
time between the movie's theatrical release and when it was shown on TV

2,300 SEQUINS
covered each ruby slipper shoe

5 PAIRS
of ruby slippers known to have been made for the movie

PRESIDENTIAL **PETS**

You've heard of the First Lady, but how about the First Pet?
Presidents Theodore Roosevelt and John F. Kennedy had some of the quirkiest pets
of all the presidents, partly because both had children who were living at the White
House at the time. See which president gets more votes in this pet lineup.

JOHN F. KENNEDY
35th president of
the United States

2 PARAKEETS

5 HORSES

5 DOGS

2 HAMSTERS

1 CANARY

1 CAT

1 RABBIT

THEODORE ROOSEVELT

26th president of the United States

1 BARN OWL

1 BLUE MACAW

(AT LEAST) 5 DOGS

2 CATS

1 PONY

1 BADGER

1 PIG

1 ROOSTER

1 BLACK BEAR

1 HYENA

5 GUINEA PIGS

1 RABBIT

1 LIZARD

153

MILKSHAKE MADNESS

Who doesn't love a thick, creamy milkshake? Get out your straw and dive into these facts about this sweet dairy treat.

THE ARTIFICIAL FLAVOR USED IN SOME STRAWBERRY MILKSHAKES CONTAINS ABOUT

40

DIFFERENT CHEMICALS.

A CHEF IN NEW YORK MADE A

6,000–
(22,713 L)

GALLON MILKSHAKE, WHICH IS THE SAME AS

48,000

NORMAL SIZE (16-oz) MILKSHAKES.

A MILKSHAKE STRAW IS

0.3
(7.6 mm)

INCH IN DIAMETER AND NEARLY

8
(20 cm)

INCHES LONG.

EVERY AMERICAN EATS ON AVERAGE

18.7

POUNDS (8.5 kg) OF ICE CREAM EVERY YEAR.

A SMALL MCDONALD'S VANILLA MILKSHAKE HAS

530

CALORIES AND **8** GRAMS OF PROTEIN.

IT WOULD TAKE

5.28 million

16-OZ (0.5-L) MILKSHAKES TO FILL AN OLYMPIC-SIZE SWIMMING POOL.

Some of these animals have a long way to go before reaching their seasonal home. See just how far some animals migrate as a regular part of their life cycles.

LEATHERBACK TURTLE
FROM NEW GUINEA

TO KENYA

FROM TANZANIA

PLAINS ZEBRAS

Distance:
300 MILES
(480 km)

Why: To follow the rains as they water the lush grasses they eat

TO COASTAL
CALIFORNIA
AND OREGON

MONARCH BUTTERFLIES

FROM CANADA

Distance:
3,000 MILES
(4,800 km)

Why: To reach their
warm winter home

Distance:
6,500 MILES
(10,460 km)
Why: To reach their
nesting beaches

TO MEXICO

ARCTIC TERN
Distance:

**25,000
MILES** (40,000 km)

Why:
To reach
breeding
grounds

FROM ANTARCTICA

TO THE ARCTIC

PIÑATA POWER

Piñatas are world travelers and have had their place in China, Italy, and beyond. But mostly they're known for the treats inside! So after you smash yours and gorge on the candy inside, check out these shattering facts on some awesome modern-day piñatas.

THE PIÑATA APPLE—A CROSS BETWEEN 3 DIFFERENT KINDS OF APPLES—WAS NAMED APPLE OF THE YEAR IN GERMANY IN 2001.

SOME TRADITIONAL PIÑATAS HAVE 7 POINTS TO SYMBOLIZE THE 7 DEADLY SINS.

504 PIÑATAS
WORLD RECORD FOR LARGEST PIÑATA DISPLAY IN HERMOSILLO, MEXICO

5,000 HOURS
46-FOOT (14-M)-TALL ORANGE PRETZEL M&M PIÑATA TO CELEBRATE THE CANDY'S FIRST "BIRTHDAY" IN 2011
HOW LONG IT TOOK TO CREATE A

8,000 POUNDS (3,628 KG)
THE WEIGHT OF CANDY FILLING A RECORD-SETTING **59-FOOT** (18-M)- **94-FOOT** (29-M)-LONG, TALL DONKEY PIÑATA IN PHILADELPHIA, PENNSYLVANIA, U.S.A.

37 ARTISTS
WERE FEATURED IN A **2011** PIÑATA EXHIBIT AT A MEXICO CITY, MEXICO, ART MUSEUM

SKATING **ON WATER**

Pro skateboarder Bob Burnquist really caught some big air on this floating (yes, floating!) skateboard ramp near D. L. Bliss State Park in Lake Tahoe, California, U.S.A. Get ready for an adrenaline rush and find out what it took to build this amazing contraption.

Bob has **26** X Games medals—more than anyone else.

7,300 POUNDS
WEIGHT OF FINAL RAMP (3,311 KG)

Bob turned pro when he was **14 years old.**

The floating skate park was made up of **2 ramps:** 1 wooden bank was **8 feet** (2.4 M) tall, and the smaller one was **5 feet** (1.5 M) in height.

36 FEET (11 M)
LENGTH OF THE FLOATING RAMP

300 HOURS

TIME IT TOOK TO BUILD THE PLATFORM

 1,250 SCREWS

WERE NEEDED TO PUT IT TOGETHER

It took **4 hours** going at about **4 knots** (7 km/h) to tow the floating ramp to its final location.

WHAT'S FOR LUNCH?

PB&J anyone? American kids head for the basics when it comes to the inside of their lunch boxes. Dig in to these numbers to find out what percentage of 6- to 12-year-olds' homemade lunches contain these items.

THE AMOUNT OF PEANUT BUTTER AMERICANS EAT EACH YEAR COULD MAKE MORE THAN **10 BILLION** PEANUT BUTTER AND JELLY SANDWICHES.

FRUIT DRINKS:
28%

FRESH FRUIT:
48%

SANDWICHES:
66%

SNACK BARS: **10%**

FRUIT SNACKS: **8%**

SALTY SNACKS: **33%**

VEGETABLES: **9%**

COOKIES: **12%**

YOGURT: **11%**

CRACKERS: **12%**

THE AVERAGE STRAWBERRY HAS **200** SEEDS.

THE WORLD'S LARGEST CHOCOLATE CHIP COOKIE EVER MADE WAS MORE THAN **100 FEET** (30 M) WIDE.

If you could jump in a spaceship and travel at the speed of light—186,000 miles a second (299,338 km/s)—you'd be able to go to distant worlds! Check out how long your flight would be as you departed from Earth and traveled through the solar system.

36.3 MINUTES

4.4 MINUTES

1.3 SECONDS

MOON

MARS

JUPITER

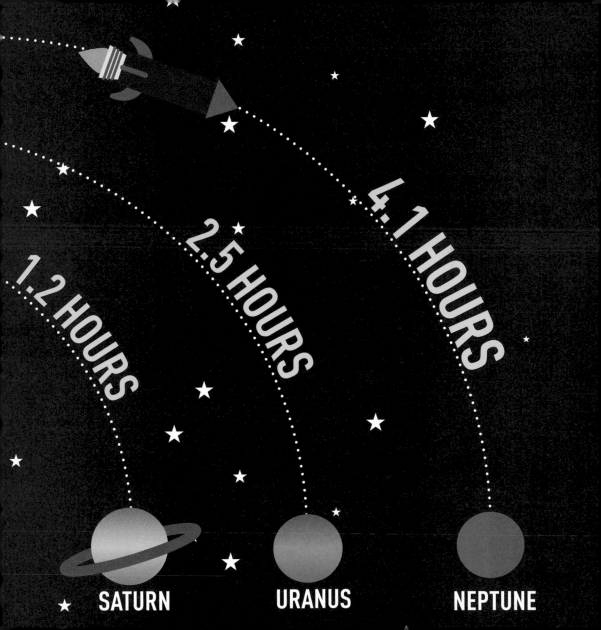

1.2 HOURS

2.5 HOURS

4.1 HOURS

SATURN

URANUS

NEPTUNE

WAY TO BE WIRED

Who out there is connected? Billions are hooked up to the Internet and hop online from a variety of different sources. Check out how 12- and 13-year-olds in the United States go online—these numbers may surprise you!

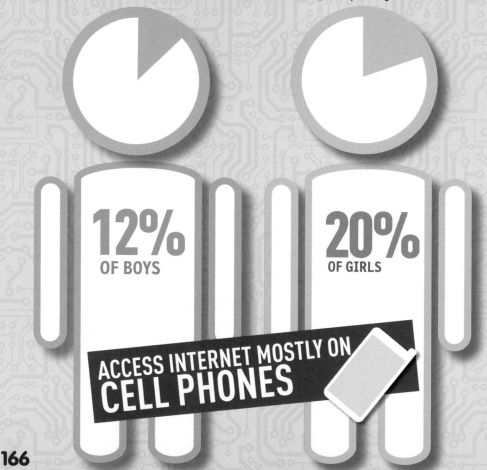

12% OF BOYS

20% OF GIRLS

ACCESS INTERNET MOSTLY ON
CELL PHONES

96% OF BOYS & 91% OF GIRLS

HAVE INTERNET ACCESS

23% OF BOYS

OWN A TABLET

28% OF GIRLS

66% OF BOYS 79% OF GIRLS

OWN A COMPUTER

5-SECOND **COUNTDOWN**

Your snack just slid off your plate and fell on the floor. Do you follow the "5-second rule"—a theory that food can't get covered in too many germs if you pick it up in less than 5 seconds—or do you toss it? Find out if your call matches that of other Americans in these survey results.

DEPENDS
ON THE ITEM
53%

RESEARCHERS IN ENGLAND RECENTLY FOUND THAT THERE'S SOME TRUTH BEHIND THE 5-SECOND RULE. THEIR STUDY SHOWED THAT FOOD

NO WAY
21%

WHAT'S THE 5-SECOND RULE?
11%

YES
(IF NO ONE STEPS ON IT)
8%

7% IT DOESN'T MATTER
5 SECONDS OR EVEN LONGER

PICKED UP JUST A FEW SECONDS AFTER IT IS DROPPED IS LESS LIKELY TO CONTAIN BACTERIA THAN IF IT IS LEFT FOR LONGER PERIODS.

KINGDOM OF CORAL

Coral reefs teem with life. Fish dart between colorful anemones, green sea turtles glide through the water, octopuses hide in crevasses, and sharks are on patrol looking for a snack. And that's just for starters—get to know coral reefs better with these numbers.

100s of years

HOW LONG a coral polyp can live

850 million

PEOPLE that live within 62 MILES (100 km) of a coral reef

1/4

of all species of fish live around coral reefs.

1,430 miles
(2,300 km)

LENGTH of the Great Barrier Reef along Australia's east coast

96,500 square miles
(250,000 sq km)

SIZE of the entire world's coral reefs—about the size of the U.S. state of Michigan, but only 1 PERCENT of the total ocean floor

THE GREAT BARRIER REEF IS MADE UP OF SOME 3,000 CORAL REEFS, 300 CORAL CAYS, AND 600 ISLANDS.

IT'S ALSO A HOME FOR ANIMALS, INCLUDING MORE THAN 30 SPECIES OF DOLPHINS AND WHALES, 500 KINDS OF WORMS, MORE THAN 100 SPECIES OF JELLYFISH, MORE THAN 1,600 KINDS OF FISH, AND 133 SHARKS AND RAYS.

Check out the figures on these lovable pets to decide for yourself.

MEOW!

Cats have been domesticated for at least **4,000 years.**

The average life span of an indoor cat is **13 to 17 years.**

People in the United States own **95.6 million** cats.

The average cat owner spends about **$1,200 a year** on a kitty.

Cats can hear sounds almost **1.5 times higher** than dogs can hear.

Cats sleep about **15 hours** a day.

PET CATS ARE RELATED TO COUGARS.

ALL KITTENS ARE BORN WITH BLUE EYES.

WOOF!

Dogs have been domesticated for at least **14,000 years.**

The average life span of a dog is **8 to 16 years.**

People in the United States own **83.3 million** dogs.

The average dog owner spends about **$1,600 a year** on a pup.

Dogs have about **220 million** scent cells—20 times more than cats.

Dogs sleep about **14 hours** a day.

NEWBORN PUPPIES DON'T WAG **THEIR** TAILS.

DOGS ARE RELATED TO WOLVES.

A WATERMELON IS
92%
WATER

The WORLD RECORD for greatest spitting distance of a watermelon seed is

THE WORLD'S
HEAVIEST
WATERMELON WEIGHED
268.8
POUNDS.
(121.93 KG)

75 FEET, 2 INCHES (23 M)—that's the same length as **12.5 picnic tables.**

Watermelons appear in hieroglyphics found on the walls of Egyptian ruins more than **5,000 years old.**

ADDING UP THE OPERA HOUSE

The world-famous Sydney Opera House in Sydney, Australia, hosts some 40 shows every week, from opera and theatre to rock concerts and dance. It's also jam-packed with numbers.

MORE THAN **1,000,000** ROOF TILES

HIGHEST ROOF SHELL (OR SAIL) **220** FEET (67 M)

ABOVE SEA LEVEL, AS TALL AS A 22-STORY BUILDING

COST TO BUILD: **$102,000,000** AUSTRALIAN DOLLARS*

* That's $80,205,150 in US dollars today.

THE CONCERT HALL ORGAN HAS **10,154** PIPES

15,500 LIGHTBULBS ARE REPLACED EVERY YEAR.

1,000 ROOMS **2,679** SEATS IN THE CONCERT HALL.

It took **14** years and **10,000** construction workers to build the Opera House; it was expected to only take **4** years.

AIR CONDITIONER
FOR 3 HOURS A DAY
$109.51

CEILING FAN FOR 3
HOURS A DAY
$8.21

INCANDESCENT LIGHT
BULB FOR 5 HOURS A DAY
$10.95

LAPTOP USED FOR
2 HOURS A DAY
$4.38

GAME CONSOLE FOR
1 HOUR A DAY
$3.29

POWER **UP!**

Ever wondered how much it costs to run your computer or dry your hair? Take a look at how your average energy use contributes to your family's power bill each year.

COMPACT FLUORESCENT LIGHTBULB FOR 5 HOURS A DAY
$2.56

CELL PHONE CHARGER
Left plugged in, not charging
$0.44

ALARM CLOCK RADIO
$1.75

HAIR DRYER FOR 10 MINUTES A DAY
$9.12

VACUUMING FOR 10 MINUTES A DAY
$8.51

179

IT WOULD TAKE A STACK OF
121 TAJ MAHALS
TO STRETCH FROM SEA LEVEL TO THE TOP OF **MOUNT EVEREST.**

HOLIDAY MOVIE **FAVORITES**

'Tis the season!

Watching a holiday movie can fill you with just as much cheer as eggnog or a sweet candy cane. A recent survey of Americans' favorite animated holiday movies and TV specials revealed that not even the Grinch could steal the number one spot!

OTHER
6%

FROSTY THE SNOWMAN
6%

SANTA CLAUS IS COMIN' TO TOWN
8%

THE POLAR EXPRESS
11%

HOW THE GRINCH STOLE CHRISTMAS!
19%

RUDOLPH THE RED-NOSED REINDEER

24%

A CHARLIE BROWN CHRISTMAS

24%

EIFFEL TOWER TRIVIA

When you hear Paris, France, what do you think of? If you immediately thought of the impressive Eiffel Tower, you are not alone. The iron tower has symbolized the great city of Paris since 1889, when it opened at the World's Fair. But how well do you really know it?

Height: **1,063 feet** (324 m)

7 million people visit each year.

Construction took **2 years, 2 months, and 5 days.**

Each night for up to **10 minutes** every hour, **20,000 bulbs** make the tower shine.

To install the light bulbs, **25 mountain climbers** were hired to do the job.

The tower's elevators travel more than **64,000 miles** [103,000 km] each year—that's more than **2.5 times** around the world!

Dare to take the stairs? There are **1,665 steps to the top.**

185

The world's largest scoop of ice cream weighed **3,010** pounds (1,365 kg).

That's the same weight as 34 emperor penguins!

Hockey players fly past you, driving the puck to the net, during a fast-paced game. Since 1893, teams have been competing for the glory of winning the sport's biggest prize, the Stanley Cup. Here is how teams playing today stack up in Cups won.

24 MONTREAL CANADIENS

11 DETROIT RED WINGS

14 TORONTO MAPLE LEAFS

6 BOSTON BRUINS

5 EDMONTON OILERS

5 CHICAGO BLACKHAWKS

4
NY RANGERS

4
NY ISLANDERS

3
NEW JERSEY
DEVILS

2
COLORADO
AVALANCHE

3
PITTSBURGH
PENGUINS

2
PHILADELPHIA
FLYERS

2
L.A. KINGS

1
CAROLINA
HURRICANES

1
TAMPA BAY
LIGHTNING

1
CALGARY FLAMES

1
ANAHEIM
DUCKS

1
DALLAS STARS

STEP 1 RAILCARS ARRIVE AT THE CRAYON FACTORY FULL OF PARAFFIN WAX. THE CARS ARE HEATED WITH STEAM AND THEN THE FRESHLY MELTED WAX IS PUMPED INTO SILOS THAT HOLD

100,000 POUNDS OF WAX EACH.
(45,359 KG)

WAX

STEP 2 THE WAX IS MOVED INTO MIXING KETTLES, WHERE CHEMICALS ARE ADDED TO KEEP THE WAX FROM STICKING AND TO IMPROVE HOW THE CRAYON RUBS ONTO PAPER.

EACH **250-POUND** (113-KG) BATCH IS TINTED A SPECIFIC COLOR, THEN BLENDED.

STEP 3 THE WAX IS PUMPED INTO A MACHINE THAT INJECTS THE WAX INTO 110 MOLDS.

AFTER THEY COOL, A ROBOTIC ARM MOVES THEM TO A LABELING STATION.

STEP 4 WHEN THE CRAYONS MOVE ON TO PACKAGING, A COLLATING MACHINE SORTS THE COLORS, ALLOWING ONLY 1 CRAYON OF EACH COLOR INTO A BOX.

STEP 5 A LASER CODE IS ADDED TO EVERY BOX AND THE CRAYONS ARE SHIPPED TO SUPPLIERS. THE CRAYOLA CRAYON FACTORY IN PENNSYLVANIA, U.S.A., PRODUCES 12 MILLION CRAYONS EVERY DAY.

CHAMPIONS **BALL**

The penalty kicks, the shoot-outs—the FIFA 2014 World Cup was full of drama. Germany took home the trophy, while home-team Brazil struggled. And the Adidas Brazuca was the official ball. What made it so special?

MORE THAN **30** TEAMS ACROSS **3** CONTINENTS AND **600** PLAYERS TESTED THE BALL DURING ITS DEVELOPMENT.

DURING THE WORLD CUP, COLOMBIAN PLAYER JAMES RODRIGUEZ SCORED THE MOST GOALS: **6.**

THE BALL WAS MADE FROM **6** IDENTICAL PANELS SHAPED IN THE LETTER 'X' INSTEAD OF THE **20** HEXAGONAL AND **12** PENTAGONAL PANELS FOUND ON A STANDARD SOCCER BALL.

THE BALL HAD A CIRCUMFERENCE OF **27 INCHES** (69 CM).

THE BRAZUCA WEIGHED EXACTLY **0.96 LB** (437 G).

IN BRAZIL, GERMANY SCORED THE MOST GOALS OF ANY TEAM: **18.**

SPACE JUMP

On October 14, 2012, Felix Baumgartner stepped from his space capsule out into the stratosphere and plummeted back to Earth in a free fall at a dizzying speed. Explore some of the figures behind this death-defying stunt.

185
BEATS PER MINUTE
fastest heart rate recorded for Felix during the jump

2
number of manned test flights before the final flight

25.2
number of seconds of absolute weightlessness experienced

843.6
MILES AN HOUR (1,357.6 KM/H)
speed reached during free fall; faster than the speed of sound, it equals Mach 1.25.

1/10
OF A ZIPLOC BAG:
thickness of helium balloon used to raise the capsule

Height of jump:

127,852.4
FEET (38,969.4 M)

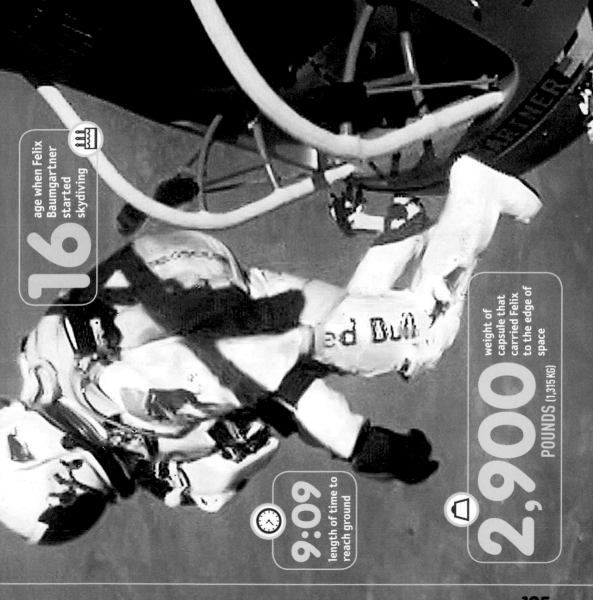

16 age when Felix Baumgartner started skydiving

2,900 POUNDS (1,315 KG) weight of capsule that carried Felix to the edge of space

9:09 length of time to reach ground

195

Q: HOW DID YOU GET INVOLVED IN MATH AND NUMBERS?

A: I have always loved working with others to solve problems. I realized that there are so many people like me who want to use their passion for math and computers to make the world better, so I started a nonprofit called DataKind that does exactly that. For example, we have used data to map poverty in different areas so that we can better understand how and where to help.

Q: WHAT DO YOU LOVE ABOUT NUMBERS?

A: Some people think math is boring, but numbers help us learn about our world. For me, numbers and math are the skills that I have learned to use in the fight for good.

Q: HOW DO PEOPLE BENEFIT FROM YOUR WORK?

A: Think of all the things computers help you with every day— your homework, plus other activities. Numbers also have the power to do much more. Computers, math, and numbers have the power to fight villains like hunger and poverty around the world and that's what I am working to achieve.

Q: FILL IN THE BLANK: MATH IS _____.

A: My favorite superpower! (Ok, other than flying ... and an invisibility cloak.)

EXTREME CLIMATES

Talk about a temperature swing! The difference between the coldest place on Earth—east Antarctica—and the hottest—Death Valley, in Nevada and California, U.S.A.—is a whopping 270 degrees Fahrenheit (150 degrees Celsius). Though they are both deserts, these two opposites are neck and neck in the race for world's most extreme climate.

HOT DEATH VALLEY

CRAZY TEMPS	Hottest temperature ever recorded: **134°F** (57°C)
RAINFALL	Death Valley is the driest place in North America. The average yearly rainfall is about **2 inches** (5 cm).
ELEVATION	At **282 feet below sea level** (-86 m), Death Valley is the lowest point in North America.
STEADY HEAT	In 2001, Death Valley experienced **160 consecutive days** of temperatures **100 degrees F** (38°C) or hotter.

EAST ANTARCTIC PLATEAU COLD

CRAZY TEMPS	Coldest temperature ever recorded: **-135.8°F** (Recorded with remote-sensing satellites) (-93°C)
RAINFALL	East Antarctica gets less than **2 inches** (5 cm) of precipitation in a year.
ELEVATION	The record low temperature was recorded just below the plateau's **13,000-foot** (3,962-m) ridge.
DARKNESS	During parts of winter, there is **24 hours** of darkness.

SPORTS SHOWDOWN

Play ball! But should you play soccer, baseball, or football?

A poll asked 12- to 17-year-old Americans whether they were an avid fan of specific professional or college sports. The National Football League notched the most fans (though kids could choose more than 1 sport). Check out the scoreboard to see how all the sports fared.

NATIONAL FOOTBALL LEAGUE
39%

NATIONAL BASKETBALL ASSOCIATION
30%

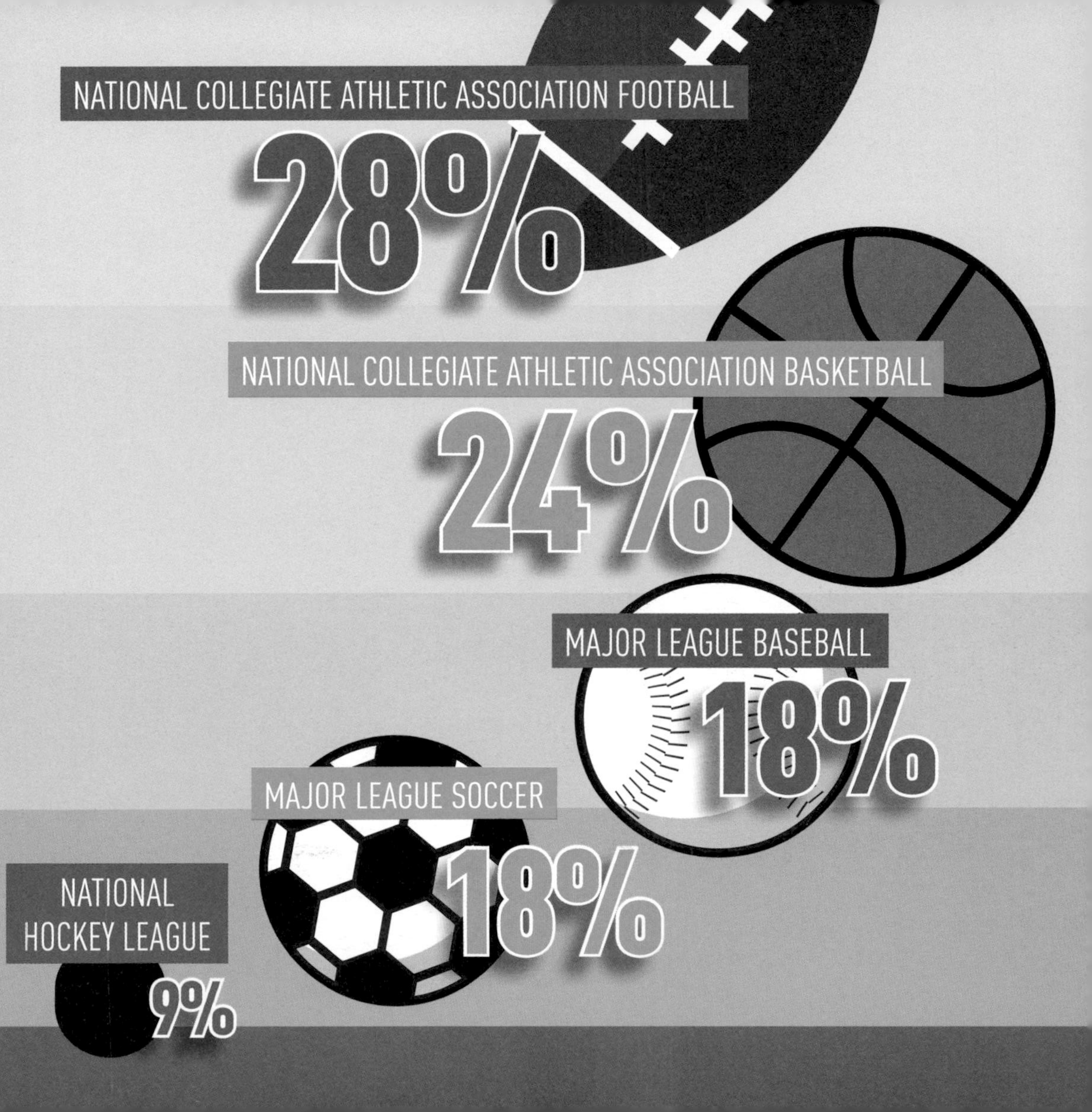

NATIONAL COLLEGIATE ATHLETIC ASSOCIATION FOOTBALL

28%

NATIONAL COLLEGIATE ATHLETIC ASSOCIATION BASKETBALL

24%

MAJOR LEAGUE BASEBALL

18%

MAJOR LEAGUE SOCCER

18%

NATIONAL HOCKEY LEAGUE

9%

5% OTHER, SUCH AS GEOTHERMAL, SOLAR, WIND, HEAT, ETC.

5% OIL

10.9% NUCLEAR

Worldwide, the Internet uses about the same amount of electricity as is generated by 30 nuclear power plants.

16.2% HYDRO POWER

40.4%
COAL

22.5%
NATURAL GAS

It seems like we use electricity for everything—from TVs and cell phones to air conditioners and computers. In fact, power plants generate 3.7 times more electrical power than they did just 40 years ago. How they do this can differ around the world. Is it from burning coal or taming the energy in moving water? Here's the global breakdown.

Electricity travels at the speed of light—about 186,000 miles (299,330 km) a second.

CIVILIZATION CALENDAR

People in ancient cultures developed writing and the wheel; they started to farm and domesticated animals; and they built huge pyramids and monuments. But you might be surprised to see some ancient cultures overlapped. Here are dates for a few cultures that have stood the test of time.

SUMERIANS	3500 TO 2340 B.C.
ANCIENT EGYPT	3100 TO 30 B.C.
INDUS VALLEY	2500 TO 1500 B.C.
AKKADIAN EMPIRE	2370 TO 1900 B.C.
MINOANS	2000 TO 1500 B.C.
BABYLONIAN	1900 TO 1100 B.C.

ANCIENT GREECE	1100 TO 50 B.C.
ANCIENT ROME	753 TO A.D. 312
MOCHE	400 TO A.D. 600
OLMEC	1500 TO 300 B.C.
ANCIENT INDIA	1500 TO 500 B.C.
CLASSIC MAYA	A.D. 350 TO 950
INCA	1100 TO 1534

A.D. 2000
A.D. 1500
A.D. 1000
A.D. 500
0
500 B.C.
1000 B.C.
1500 B.C.
2000 B.C.
2500 B.C.
3000 B.C.
3500 B.C.

BATTLE OF **THE DOLLS**

Sure they've been dating forever, and sure they make a cute couple, but how do Barbara Millicent Rogers (aka Barbie) and Ken Carson really stack up—face-to-face?

BARBIE

 BIRTHDAY: MARCH 9, 1959

 HEIGHT: 11.5 INCHES (29 CM)

 CAREERS: 150 (RAN FOR PRESIDENT MORE THAN 6 TIMES)

 HAIR COLORS: 7 DIFFERENT SHADES OF BLONDE

 SIBLINGS: 3 SISTERS

More than 100 people are involved in making each of Barbie's outfits.

Barbie traveled into space in 1965, 4 years before astronauts landed on the moon.

I AM REALLY ROCKING THIS HAIRSTYLE!

KEN

 BIRTHDAY: MARCH 11, 1961

 HEIGHT: 12 INCHES (31 CM)

 CAREERS: BEST KNOWN AS AN ACTOR, DEBUTED IN *TOY STORY 3* AND HAD 50 COSTUME CHANGES

 HAIR COLORS: 9

 SIBLINGS: 1 BROTHER

Barbie and Ken broke up in 2004 (on Valentine's Day), but got back together 7 years later.

AMAZING GAMING **HISTORY**

Playing the latest hottest game?

Around the world, people spend 3 billion hours a week playing video games. But where did it all start? See how far we've come in this timeline of video game developments.

1978 Space Invaders is released, a game where you have to fight **48 aliens** in 6 columns to get to the next stage.

1972 The first home video game console, the Magnavox Odyssey, sets the wheels in motion. It sold **330,000 units.**

1980 Pac-Man hits the scene. In this game, PacMan has to eat up all **240 dots** on the screen before 4 hungry ghosts catch him. The highest number of points it's possible to score is **3,333,360.**

1983 Nintendo's Family Computer was the first console to let players save their scores.

1989 Nintendo's Game Boy enters the market, with Tetris included. Worldwide, over **150 million** systems have been sold.

1995 Sony released the PlayStation game console in the United States. More than **100,000** are sold in the first weekend.

1999 Sega's Dreamcast hits the stores on September 9, 1999. Within 24 hours it sells nearly **$100 million** worth of software and hardware.

2001 Microsoft gets into the game with the Xbox; Nintendo releases GameCube.

2005 Guitar Hero released. After **6 years** and 19 different "Hero" games, the series ends.

2006 In the span of 2 days, the Sony PlayStation 3 and Nintendo Wii hit the stores in the U.S.

2011 The game Minecraft is officially released. By 2015, more than **19 million** people have bought the game.

COMPUTING **POWER**

The first computer, ENIAC, weighed **30 tons** (27 t).

That's as much as **12 white rhinos!**

LET IT SNOW

Brrr! It snows all over the world, but how much will you get? Check out what annual snowfall amounts would look like if the snow were marshmallows in hot chocolate.

 = 1 foot (0.3 M) of snow

BUFFALO, NEW YORK 8 FEET (2 M)

BEIJING, CHINA 1 FOOT (0.3 M)

WHISTLER, CANADA 14 FEET (4 M)

SALZBURG, AUSTRIA 4 FEET (1.2 M)

SAPPORO, JAPAN 17 FEET (5 M)

MOSCOW, RUSSIA 5 FEET (1.5 M)

BUENOS AIRES,
ARGENTINA
0 FEET
(0 M)

JOHANNESBURG,
SOUTH AFRICA
0.008 FOOT
(0.002 M)

SOUTH POLE,
ANTARCTICA
0.7 FOOT
(0.2 M)

CHIONOPHOBIA IS THE FEAR OF SNOW.

THE AVERAGE SNOWFLAKE FALLS AT ABOUT 3 MILES AN HOUR. (5 KM/H)

ORANGE SNOW ONCE FELL IN RUSSIA, SAID TO BE THE RESULT OF A SANDSTORM FROM NEARBY KAZAKHSTAN.

10 INCHES (30 CM) OF SNOW EQUALS ABOUT 1 INCH (3 CM) OF WATER IN MOST PARTS OF THE WORLD.

213

LEGO **AHOY!**

In 1997, a container ship was hit by a massive wave west of England, dumping nearly 4.8 million Lego pieces into the sea. Since then, many of them have been washing up on English shores, where beachcombers have taken to collecting them. Check out the amazing numbers on these building blocks that keep drifting ashore—even today!

418,000
DIVER FLIPPERS

33,941
DRAGONS

97,500
SCUBA AND BREATHING APPARATUSES

A total of **4,756,940** Lego pieces went overboard.

It's estimated that only **3,178,807** of the lost pieces are light enough to float.

353,264 DAISY FLOWERS

13,000 SPEAR GUNS

4,200 BLACK OCTOPUSES

26,400 BROWN SHIP RIGGING NETS

26,600 YELLOW LIFE PRESERVERS

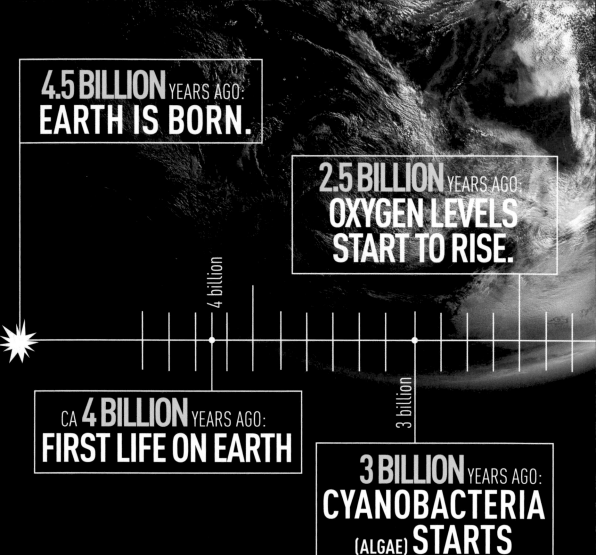

4.5 BILLION YEARS AGO:
EARTH IS BORN.

2.5 BILLION YEARS AGO:
**OXYGEN LEVELS
START TO RISE.**

4 billion

3 billion

CA **4 BILLION** YEARS AGO:
FIRST LIFE ON EARTH

3 BILLION YEARS AGO:
**CYANOBACTERIA
(ALGAE) STARTS**

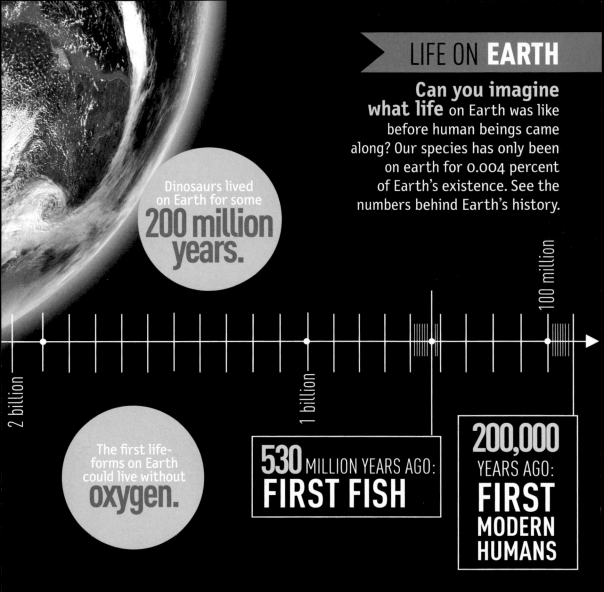

LIFE ON **EARTH**

Can you imagine what life on Earth was like before human beings came along? Our species has only been on earth for 0.004 percent of Earth's existence. See the numbers behind Earth's history.

Dinosaurs lived on Earth for some **200 million years.**

The first life-forms on Earth could live without **oxygen.**

100 million

2 billion

1 billion

530 MILLION YEARS AGO: **FIRST FISH**

200,000 YEARS AGO: **FIRST MODERN HUMANS**

217

BRAIN POWER

Your brain is the tops—literally.

It's the most complex organ in your body, an amazing supercomputer that controls everything you do. Check out some incredible info behind the numbers that nourish your noggin.

LIKE THE EARTH, YOUR BRAIN IS DIVIDED INTO

2

HEMISPHERES.

YOUR BRAIN CAN HOLD

1 MILLION

GIGABYTES OF DATA. IF YOUR BRAIN WAS LIKE A DVR, IT COULD HOLD **3 MILLION** HOURS OF TELEVISION SHOWS.

YOUR BRAIN CONTAINS

BILLIONS

OF NERVE CELLS.

THE BRAIN HAS

12

NERVE PAIRS THAT CONTROL THINGS LIKE TASTE AND HEARING.

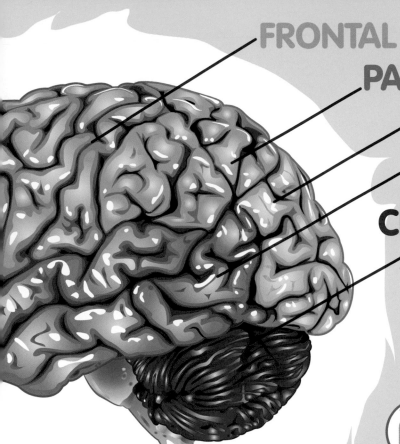

FRONTAL

PARIETAL

OCCIPITAL

TEMPORAL

CEREBELLUM

ABOUT
2/3
OF YOUR BRAIN IS
MADE UP OF
SPECIALIZED FATS.

YOUR BRAIN IS ABOUT **6 INCHES** LONG.
(15 CM)

YOUR BRAIN
WEIGHS ABOUT
3 POUNDS.
(1 KG)

YEAR OF THE **PLANET**

Watch the world spin! It takes Earth a little over 365 days, or 1 year, to rotate around the sun. But for the solar system's other planets, the trip looks a little different. See how many Earth days or years it takes for other planets to orbit.

It takes our sun about **250 million** years to orbit the center of the Milky Way galaxy.

Neptune has only completed one full orbit, in **2011**, since its **1846** discovery.

One day on Venus lasts **243** Earth days—so Venus' day is longer than its year!

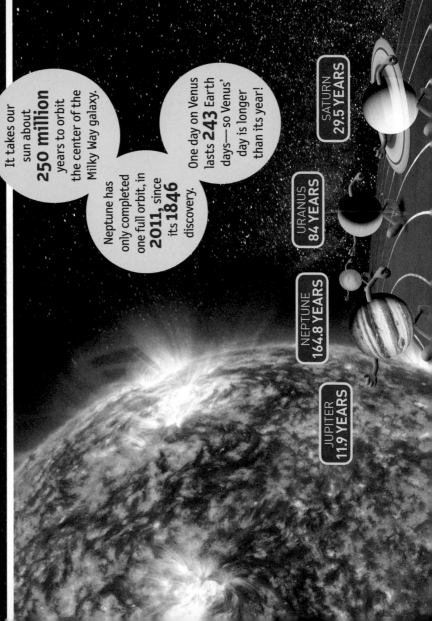

SATURN
29.5 YEARS

URANUS
84 YEARS

NEPTUNE
164.8 YEARS

JUPITER
11.9 YEARS

VENUS
224.7 DAYS

MARS
1.9 YEARS

EARTH
1 YEAR

MERCURY
88 DAYS

It's the last seconds

of the game and your favorite NBA player is at the free throw line. Will he choke? Or will he clinch the title? If this basketball star pays attention to these mathematical free throw tips scientists found, it'll be a slam dunk!

DIAMETER OF BASKETBALL:

9.4 INCHES
(23.9 CM)

6 FEET 6 INCHES
(2 M)

LAUNCH THE BASKETBALL AT A

52 °ANGLE.

DISTANCE BETWEEN THE FREE THROW LINE AND BACKBOARD:

15 FEET
(5 M)

222

MAKE SURE TO GIVE THE BALL BACKSPIN OF AT LEAST

3

REVOLUTIONS PER SECOND.

DIAMETER OF THE RIM:

18 INCHES

(46 CM)

DON'T AIM FOR THE CENTER OF THE BASKET BUT A SPOT

2.8 INCHES (7 CM)

BACK FROM THE CENTER OF THE BASKET.

THE RIM IS

10 FEET (3 CM)

FROM THE GROUND.

CRUNCHING THE NUMBERS

Gooey, crunchy, crispy, or colorful—every brand of chocolate bar has something different to offer. And everyone has their favorite. Here are the top chocolate bars, by units sold in the United States.

60,808,770

73,445,960

80,053,290

94,410,500

161,715,900

192,127,200

249,449,600

347,164,400

383,687,900

407,409,600

The world's largest chocolate bar weighed

12,770 pounds.
(5,792 kg)   That's as much as an elephant!

RAPTOR TAKEDOWN

Neither the great horned owl nor the turkey vulture is a raptor that should be messed with. The great horned owl catches its prey on the run while the turkey vulture starts circling at the first sign of death. But which one is the ultimate bird of prey? Snatch up these numbers and find out.

GREAT HORNED OWL
BIGGEST OWL IN NORTH AMERICA

WEIGHT: UP TO **88 OZ** (3 KG)

WINGSPAN: UP TO **57 INCHES** (145 CM)

FLIGHT SPEED: UP TO **40 MPH** (64 KM/H)

CLAIM TO FAME: CAN SWIVEL ITS HEAD MORE THAN **270°**

WHEN CLENCHED, ITS TALONS REQUIRE **28 LBS** OF FORCE (13 KG) TO OPEN.

TURKEY VULTURE
SUPER SCAVENGER

WEIGHT: UP TO **70** OZ (2 KG)

WINGSPAN: UP TO **70 INCHES** (178 CM)

FLIGHT SPEED: UP TO **60 MPH** (97 KM/H)

CLAIM TO FAME: CAN SMELL CARRION MORE THAN **1 MILE** (1.6 KM) AWAY

HAS BEEN KNOWN TO TRAVEL UP TO **200 MILES** (322 KM) A DAY AND HAS BEEN SEEN FLYING AT **20,000 FEET** (6,100 M)

Did you know it takes more than a cup of water to make a cup of coffee?

In fact, it takes 35 gallons (132 L)! Water isn't just used to brew java; it's also used to grow and process the coffee beans. The same goes for all the food we eat. Check out how much water is used to produce your favorite chow.

 = 5 Gallons (20 L)

10 GALLONS (38 L)

13 GALLONS (49 L)

18 GALLONS (70 L)

50 GALLONS (189 L)

110 GALLONS (416 L)

1 SLICE OF BREAD

1 ORANGE

1 APPLE

1 EGG

1 LB CORN (455 G)

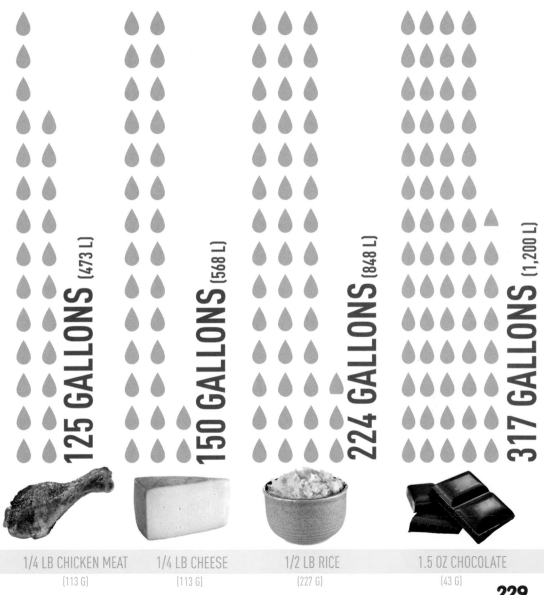

125 GALLONS (473 L)

150 GALLONS (568 L)

224 GALLONS (848 L)

317 GALLONS (1,200 L)

1/4 LB CHICKEN MEAT (113 G)

1/4 LB CHEESE (113 G)

1/2 LB RICE (227 G)

1.5 OZ CHOCOLATE (43 G)

SUPER CAVE

Hidden deep in the dense mountain jungle of Vietnam is a massive underworld, Hang Son Doong cave. No other cavern in the world comes close to matching it in total size. Explore the world's largest cave, with its towering cliffs and staggering sights, in this awesome infographic.

THIS IS A PERSON!

More than **600 feet** (183 m):
cavern height in some sections

5.5 miles (8.9 km):
total length of cave

This explorer is standing on a formation called Hand of the Dog, more than 0.5 mile (805 m) away from where this picture was taken.

2.2 miles (3.5 km): total length of main passage (where this was taken)

Nearly **500 feet** (152 m): cavern width in some sections

40-story

An entire New York City, U.S.A., block complete with 40-story skyscrapers could fit inside one of this cave's vast chambers.

Hang Son Doong was formed between **2** and **5 million** years ago by a river that carved through soft limestone rock.

Hang Son Doong is part of a network of **150** different connected caverns.

A sinkhole collapsed part of the cave's roof, bringing the jungle down into the cave and creating a "skylight." A forest with trees as tall as **100 feet** (30 m) now grows from inside the cavern. Monkeys, snakes, and birds inhabit this cave jungle.

231

Ready to speed through

Space Mountain in Disney World or take a runaway train ride at Disneyland in California? Disney amusement parks anchor the U.S. coasts—one in the West and one in the East. So strap in and get ready to learn all about the numbers behind these action-packed parks.

DISNEY WORLD

Covers about
25,600
ACRES (10,360 ha) and has 4 theme parks and 2 water parks in central Florida.

Trash cans in the Magic Kingdom are connected to a system of underground tubes that can send trash rushing up to
60 MPH
(97 km/h).

Cinderella Castle reaches
189 FEET (58 m) into the sky.

Employs some
74,000 cast members.

The Space Mountain coaster reaches speeds of
28.7 MPH
(46 km/h).

DISNEYLAND

Covers about **500 ACRES** (200 ha) and has 2 theme parks in Orange County, California.

The Matterhorn Bobsleds ride was the world's first tubular steel roller coaster, with bobsleds careening at **18 MPH** (29 km/h).

Employs **28,000** cast members.

Sleeping Beauty Castle towers **77 FEET** (23 m) above the moat below.

Disneyland recycles more than **32 TONS** (29 t) of material each day. That's the weight of a dozen Jungle Cruise boats.

RAS!

How we MADE IT

An infographic may look simple and easy to read on the page, but each piece—whether it's a fact, picture, or number—needs to be carefully thought out until it looks just right. Check out how we made these awesome infographics in *By the Numbers*.

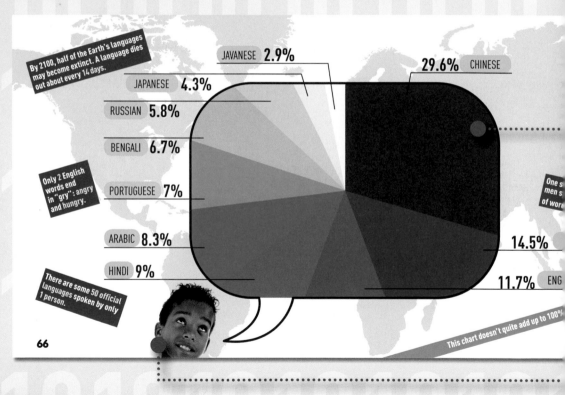

By 2100, half of the Earth's languages may become extinct. A language dies out about every 14 days.

JAVANESE **2.9%**

29.6% CHINESE

JAPANESE **4.3%**

RUSSIAN **5.8%**

BENGALI **6.7%**

Only 2 English words end in "gry": angry and hungry.

PORTUGUESE **7%**

One s
men s
of wor

ARABIC **8.3%**

14.5%

HINDI **9%**

11.7% ENG

There are some 50 official languages spoken by only 1 person.

This chart doesn't quite add up to 100%

First, we started with a topic that was really interesting and surprising. Then our researchers looked through lots of reliable sources to find some data.

Because there are so many languages and billions of people on Earth who speak them, we decided to simplify the data and focus on the top 10 world languages. We wrote a little explanatory text to tell you exactly what you're looking at and why it matters.

The most important part of any infographic is accuracy, so every infographic in this book was checked by a data expert. In this pie chart, each "slice" was checked to make sure that, for instance, the Arabic language slice really does make up 8.3% of the whole pie chart shape.

There's so much cool information out there! We put fun facts in lots of places to show you just how amazing each infographic topic is.

The design of an infographic is just as important as its text. To make our infographics fun, easy, and interesting to look it, we pumped them up with fun colors, cool art, and awesome photographs.

WHAT?

There are
00 languages
und the w
e people speak
ent languages,
yone has their
er the one you
baby. Here are
tages of first-
eakers for the
rld languages.

omen and
ne number
000.

bers are rounded.

67

Make your own INFOGRAPHIC
Tips and Tricks to Bring NUMBERS TO LIFE!

So, what does that list of numbers mean, exactly? Instead of making a plain old bar or pie chart for your next math or science project, think about making your stats pop with a clever information graphic (infographic)—just like the ones in this book! To make your data leap off the page in a fun way, check out *National Geographic* magazine graphics editor Matthew Twombly's tips for making your own amazing infographics.

GET TO KNOW YOUR DATA AND ASK QUESTIONS

If you didn't collect your own data, **spend some time** getting familiar with it. Do you notice any trends? What about the data is **surprising** or **interesting?** These answers will help you develop a message for your audience. Does your data make you wonder about anything? **Your reader will probably ask the same thing!**

MAKE COMPARISONS

Sometimes to truly appreciate data, you have to **compare, contrast,** and **tell the whole story.** For instance, you looked out your window and counted the number of cars that drove by in one hour—five of them were red. Well, that's neat, but what's more interesting is that you also saw just one yellow car. The story is in the relationship that car colors have to one another. Your reader won't see how popular red cars are unless you are making a comparison with other car colors.

CONSIDER LOTS OF GRAPHIC STYLES AND EXPERIMENT

Are you looking at something over time? Comparing quantities? Different graphics—such as a timeline, visual comparisons, or photographs—all have their strengths and weaknesses. Knowing when to use each is important. Plus, experimenting with different forms of visualization might give you ideas you may not have thought of originally.

MAKE IT EASY FOR YOUR AUDIENCE

All those numbers might look like a big, confusing pile, but look carefully and sort them. The goal of all design is to organize information so you can convey a clear, deliberate message to an audience. You don't want to make your readers work too hard to understand that message.

NUMBERS NOT NECESSARY

Infographics can be more than just charts and graphs. Sometimes an illustration of a subject, process, or natural phenomenon is the best way to get your message across. When comparing wingspans, for example, it's probably best to draw some wings!

EXPLAIN

Your design may have a clear message, but most of the time a little explanation can't hurt! Be sure to supply the relevant information that is necessary to understanding the graphic. Labels are crucial and explanatory text can be very helpful.

BE CREATIVE AND HAVE FUN!

Remember that infographics can come in all shapes and sizes, styles, and colors. Think outside the box for clever visual ideas. Even a funny title can grab the reader's attention. If you have fun making it, you can bet everyone will have fun reading it!

Want MORE?

Grab a parent and together check out these other great resources to see and learn more about infographics and design, plus awesome stats and facts.

IN PRINT

Cook, Gareth, ed. *The Best American Infographics.* New York: Houghton Mifflin Harcourt, 2014.

Kidd, Chip. *Go: A Kidd's Guide to Graphic Design.* New York: Workman, 2013.

The Listomaniacs. *Listomania: A World of Fascinating Facts in Graphic Detail.* New York: Harper Design, 2011.

National Geographic Kids. *Weird But True!* Washington, D.C.: National Geographic, 2009– .

Rogers, Simon. *Information Graphics: Animal Kingdom.* Somerville, MA: Big Picture Press, 2014.

_____. *Information Graphics: Human Body.* Somerville, MA: Big Picture Press, 2014.

_____. *Information Graphics: Space.* Somerville, MA: Big Picture Press, 2015.

ONLINE

Daily Infographic
dailyinfographic.com
A site that features a new infographic each day on a variety of subjects.

National Geographic Education

natgeoed.org

Offers free and highly engaging geography, science, and social studies resources for students and educators.

National Geographic Kids

kids.nationalgeographic.com

Get fun facts, quizzes, games, videos, and more. Learn about wacky animals, the world, and all that's in it!

PBS Kids, Math Games

pbskids.org/games/math

Features a number of fun games intended to teach kids about math.

Piktochart

piktochart.com

With a parent's help, create a free account to experiment with different infographic templates.

WATCH

The Big Picture With Kal Penn

National Geographic Channel

channel.nationalgeographic.com/the-big-picture-with-kal-penn

A show that explores the unexpected—and sometimes surprising—realities in both the world at large and our own backyard, revealed by crunching the numbers and finding new ways to visualize data.

By the Numbers
SOURCES AND NOTES

Food Figures
Pages 10–11
Boyer, Renee, and Julie McKinney. "Food Storage Guidelines for Consumers," Virginia Cooperative Extension, Virginia Tech, Virginia State University, January 15, 2013. pubs.ext. vt.edu/348/348-960/348-960.html.

United States Food and Drug Administration. "Refrigerator & Freezer Storage Chart." hfda.gov/downloads/Food/FoodborneIllnessContaminants/UCM109315.pdf.

Favorite Flavors
Pages 12–13
Snibbe, Kurt. "Here's the Scoop," Orange County Register, July 24, 2013, accessed May 13, 2015. files.onset.freedom.com/ocregister/Focus/07242013_Focus2.pdf.

Interview with International Dairy Foods Association.

Pet Ownership in the U.S.A.
Pages 18–19
American Veterinary Medical Association. "U.S. Pet Ownership Statistics (2012)." avma.org/KB/Resources/Statistics/Pages/Market-research-statistics-US-pet-ownership.aspx.

Home Run Money
Pages 30–31
Blum, Ronald. "Dodgers top spender, ending Yanks' 15-year streak." The Associated Press, March 26, 2014, accessed May 12, 2015. bigstory.ap.org/article/dodgers-top-spender-ending-yanks-15-year-streak.

Petchesky, Barry. "2014 Payrolls and Salaries for Every MLB Team." Deadspin, March 26, 2014, accessed May 12, 2015. deadspin.com/2014-payrolls-and-salaries-for-every-mlb-team-1551868969.

Harry Potter Numbers That Cast a Spell
Pages 42–43
"Top 10 Most Common Complete Sentences From All 7 Books" list:

Blatt, Ben. "A Textual Analysis of The Hunger Games." Slate, November 20, 2013, accessed May 8, 2015. slate.com/articles/arts/culture-box/2013/11/hunger_games_catching_fire_a_textual_analysis_of_suzanne_collins_novels.html.

The Best Edibles
Pages 46–47
Centers for Disease Control and Prevention. "State Indicator Report on Fruits and Vegetables, 2013." Atlanta, Ga.: Centers for Disease Control and Prevention, U.S. Department of Health and Human Services, 2013. cdc.gov/nutrition/downloads/State-Indicator-Report-Fruits-Vegetables-2013.pdf.

Sense of Smell
Pages 52–53
Niimura Y., A. Matsui, and K. Touhara. 2014. "Extreme expansion of the olfactory receptor gene repertoire in African elephants and evolutionary dynamics of orthologous gene groups in 13 placental mammals." Genome Research, doi: 10.1101/gr.169532.113. genome.cshlp.org/content/early/2014/07/16/gr.169532.113.full.pdf+html.

Say What?
Pages 66–67
Lewis, M. Paul, Gary F. Simons, and Charles D. Fennig (eds.). 2015. Ethnologue: Languages of the World, Eighteenth edition. Dallas, Texas: SIL International. Online version: ethnologue.com.

Feeling the Burn
Pages 76–77
Ainsworth, B. E., W. L. Haskell, S. D. Herrmann, N. Meckes, D. R. Bassett, Jr., C. Tudor-Locke, J. L. Greer, J. Vezina, M. C. Whitt-Glover, and A. S. Leon. "The Compendium of Physical Activities Tracking Guide." Healthy Lifestyles Research Center, College of Nursing & Health Innovation, Arizona State University, accessed May 8, 2015. sites.google.com/site/compendiumofphysicalactivities.

Big Footprint
Pages 78–79
Boden, T. A., G. Marland, and R. J. Andres. 2013. "Global, Regional, and National Fossil-Fuel CO_2 Emissions." Carbon Dioxide Information Analysis Center, Oak Ridge National Laboratory, U.S. Department of Energy, Oak Ridge, Tenn., U.S.A. doi 10.3334/CDIAC/00001_V2013. cdiac.ornl.gov/trends/emis/overview_2010.html.

Pizza or Fufu?
Pages 84–85
Oxfam: Grow Campaign 2011. "Global Opinion Research–Final Topline Report." oxfamnovib.nl/Redactie/Downloads/Rapporten/finalgrowcampaign globescanresearchmainpresentation.pdf.

Germ Showdown
Pages 96–97
Mela, Saran, and David E. Whitworth. "The fist bump: A more hygienic alternative to the handshake," American Journal of Infection Control (2014); 42: 916–7.

Sci-Fi Factors
Pages 98–99
Centives, 2012. "How much would it cost to build the death star?" centives.net/S/2012/how-much-would-it-cost-to-build-the-death-star

Is Bigfoot Real?/Is the Loch Ness Monster Real?
Pages 108–109
"Americans More Likely to Believe in Bigfoot than Canadians," March 4, 2012, Angus Reid Public Opinion. angusreidglobal.com/wp-content/uploads/2012/03/2012.03.04_Myths.pdf.

All Aboard!
Pages 118–119
World Tourism Organization. "UNWTO Tourism Highlights, 2014 Edition." mkt.unwto.org/publication/unwto-tourism-highlights-2014-edition.

Note: All data from 2013.

Hometown Hoops
Pages 120–121
Kovar, Mykel. "The Unofficial 2014 NBA Census," Best Tickets, December 2, 2014, accessed May 12, 2015. besttickets.com/blog/unofficial-2014-nba-census.

Twister Totals
Pages 122–123
National Centers for Environmental Information. "U.S. Tornado Climatology: Average Number of Tornadoes, Averaging Period 1991-2010." ncdc.noaa.gov/climate-information/extreme-events/us-tornado-climatology.

The Sweetest Countries
Pages 124–125
International Cocoa Organization. "The World Cocoa Economy: Past and Present." icco.org/about-us/international-cocoa-agreements/cat_view/30-related-documents/45-statistics-other-statistics.html.

Note: All figures are pounds of cocoa for 2011–2012, except 2010–2011 data used for Sweden.

Pack Your Bags
Pages 126–127
World Tourism Organization. "UNWTO Tourism Highlights, 2014 Edition." unwto.org/sites/all/files/pdf/unwto_highlights14_en.pdf.

Note: All data from 2013 except for France (2012), rounded.

A Space Called Home
Pages 128–129
Pew Research Center, April 2014. "U.S. Views of Technology and the Future." pewinternet.org/2014/04/17/us-views-of-technology-and-the-future.

A Slice of the Pie
Pages 130–131
Roemmele, Brian, Quora, accessed via businessinsider.com/the-most-popular-pizza-toppings-chart-2013-10.

What's for Lunch?
Pages 162–163
"What America Eats: Our Exclusive Survey on the Nation's Changing Tastes," Parade, September 5, 2014. communitytable.com/334779/parade/what-america-eats-our-exclusive-survey-on-the-nations-changing-tastes.

Way to Be Wired
Pages 166–167
Madde, Mary, Amanda Lenhart, Maeve Duggan, Sandra Cortesi, and Urs Gasser. "Teens and Technology 2013," Pew Research Center, March 13, 2013. pewinternet.org/files/old-media/Files/Reports/2013/PIP_TeensandTechnology2013.pdf.

5-Second Countdown
Pages 168–169
"What America Eats: Our Exclusive Survey on the Nation's Changing Tastes," Parade, September 5, 2014. communitytable.com/334779/parade/what-america-eats-our-exclusive-survey-on-the-nations-changing-tastes.

Power Up!
Pages 178–179
Data sourced from energyusecalculator.com. Energy costs vary by provider; these figures use energy costs of $0.10 per kWh.

Holiday Movie Favorites
Pages 182–183
Marist Poll, maristpoll.marist.edu/tag/holiday-movies.

Ice Prize
Pages 188–189
National Hockey League. National Hockey League Official Guide & Record Book 2015. Chicago: Triumph, 2014.

Note: Montreal includes championship from 1916; some teams include franchise wins from earlier teams.

Sports Showdown
Pages 200–201
Bennett, Roger. "MLS equals MLB in popularity with kids," ESPN FC. espnfc.com/major-league-soccer/story/1740529/mls-catches-mlb-in-popularity-with-kidssays-espn-poll. March 7, 2014.

High Voltage
Pages 202–203
International Energy Agency. "Key World Energy Statistics, 2014." iea.org/publications/freepublications/publication/KeyWorld2014.pdf.

Lego Ahoy!
Pages 214–215
Cacciottolo, Mario. "The Cornish beaches where Lego keeps washing up," BBC News Magazine, July 21, 2014, accessed May 13, 2015. bbc.com/news/magazine-28367198.

The Perfect Free Throw
Pages 222–223
Tran, Chau M., and Larry M. Silverberg. "Optimal release conditions for the free throw in men's basketball," Journal of Sports Sciences 26 (September 9, 2008): 11. Accessed May 12, 2015. doi: 10.1080/02640410802004948.

Crunching the Numbers
Pages 224–225
Stockdale, Charles. "America's Favorite Chocolate Brands," 24/7 Wall St., April 5, 2012, accessed May 13, 2015. 247wallst.com/special-report/2012/04/05/americas-favorite-chocolate-brands.

Watery Menu
Pages 228–229
Water Footprint Network. "Product Gallery." waterfootprint.org/en/resources/interactive-tools/product-gallery.

INDEX

Boldface indicates illustrations.

PHOTO CREDITS

For more information, please visit nationalgeographic.com, call 1-800-NGS LINE (647-5463), or write to the following address:
National Geographic Society
1145 17th Street N.W.
Washington, D.C. 20036-4688 U.S.A.

Visit us online at nationalgeographic.com/books

For librarians and teachers: ngchildrensbooks.org

More for kids from National Geographic:
kids.nationalgeographic.com

For information about special discounts for bulk purchases, please contact National Geographic Books Special Sales:
ngspecsales@ngs.org

For rights or permissions inquiries, please contact National Geographic Books Subsidiary Rights: ngbookrights@ngs.org

Paperback ISBN: 978-1-4263-2072-9
Reinforced library binding ISBN: 978-1-4263-2073-6

Printed in the United States of America
15/QGT-CML/1

Staff for This Book
Kate Olesin, *Project Editor*
Julide Dengel, *Art Director and Designer*
Fuzzco Inc., *Designer*
Kelley Miller, *Senior Photo Editor*
Carl Mehler, *Director of Maps*
Julie Beer and Michelle Harris, *Writers*
Matthew Twombly, *Expert Consultant*
Paige Towler, *Editorial Assistant*
Erica Holsclaw, *Special Projects Assistant*
Sanjida Rashid and Rachel Kenny, *Design Production Assistants*
Michael Cassady and Mari Robinson, *Rights Clearance Specialists*
Grace Hill, *Managing Editor*
Joan Gossett, *Senior Production Editor*
Lewis R. Bassford, *Production Manager*
George Bounelis, *Manager, Production Services*
Susan Borke, *Legal and Business Affairs*

Published by the National Geographic Society
Gary E. Knell, President and CEO
John M. Fahey, Chairman of the Board
Melina Gerosa Bellows, Chief Education Officer
Declan Moore, Chief Media Officer
Hector Sierra, Senior Vice President and General Manager, Book Division

Senior Management Team, Kids Publishing and Media
Nancy Laties Feresten, *Senior Vice President;* Erica Green, *Vice President, Editorial Director, Kids Books;* Julie Vosburgh Agnone, *Vice President, Operations;* Jennifer Emmett, *Vice President, Content;* Michelle Sullivan, *Vice President, Video and Digital Initiatives;* Eva Absher-Schantz, *Vice President, Visual Identity;* Rachel Buchholz, *Editor and Vice President, NG Kids magazine;* Jay Sumner, *Photo Director;* Hannah August, *Marketing Director;* R. Gary Colbert, *Production Director*

Digital Laura Goertzel, *Manager;* Sara Zeglin, *Senior Producer;* Bianca Bowman, *Assistant Producer;* Natalie Jones, *Senior Product Manager*

FASTEST, *S L O W E S T*, TINIEST, BIGGEST, WEIRDEST, SMELLIEST, **LOUDEST,** DEADLIEST

NATIONAL GEOGRAPHIC KiDS

ANIMAL **RECORDS**

THE **BIGGEST,** *FASTEST,* GROSSEST, TINIEST, SLOWEST, AND SMELLIEST CREATURES ON THE PLANET

DEADLIEST

STRONGEST

BIGGEST

KATHY FURGANG AND SARAH WASSNER

NUMBERS come **ALIVE** in this action-packed book, filled with mind-blowing animal stats, species smack-downs, cool lists, plus fun and games.

NATIONAL GEOGRAPHIC KiDS

OCTOPUSES: BIG BRAINS AND BIG SMARTS

So you read on page 25 that octopuses are supersmart, but did you know that scientists study their brains to learn more about yours? Proportionate to size, octopuses have the largest and most complex brains of all invertebrates. Their brains are very different from ours, yet octopuses display some of the same smarts. They recognize their own names, solve puzzles, and pry open childproof jars.

By studying octopus brains, researchers think they can learn about how our own noggins store and recall information. They also hope to figure out how the eight-armed eggheads display humanlike actions while having such a unique nervous system. And perhaps they'll even discover ways that human interaction...

32

OCTOPUSES HAVE THREE HEARTS.

AN OCTOPUS BRAIN HAS ABOUT **300 MILLION NEURONS (NERVE CELLS).**

33

MAKE SOME NOISE!

Check out how these animal noises measure up to some of the loudest things in the world!

A decibel (dB) is the unit for measuring sound. The louder the noise, the higher the decibel. For example, a crying baby is about 115 dB.

ROCK CONCERT

115 dB A LION'S ROAR

= 110 dB A JAMAICAN FRUIT-EATING BAT'S SHRIEK

CHAIN SAW

A DOG'S BARK = 100 dB SUBWAY TRAIN

138

= 120 dB AMBULANCE SIREN

A CICADA'S CHIRP

A PIG'S SQUEAL = 130 dB

JACKHAMMER

A HOWLER MONKEY'S CALL

AIRPLANE TAKING OFF 140 =

139

Ever wondered what a really **TINY INFOGRAPHIC** looks like? This square represents just

0.01% OF THIS WHOLE PAGE!